# Buccaneers and Pirates

"The pirates climbed up the sides of the man-of-war as if
they had been twenty-nine cats" . . *Frontispiece*

# Buccaneers and Pirates

## Frank R. Stockton

With Illustrations by
George Varian and B. West Clinedinst

Dover Publications, Inc.
Mineola, New York

*Bibliographical Note*

This Dover edition, first published in 2007, is an unabridged republication of the work originally published by The Macmillan Company, New York, in 1908 under the title *Buccaneers and Pirates of Our Coasts* (first publication: 1898).

*Library of Congress Cataloging-in-Publication Data*

Stockton, Frank Richard, 1834–1902.
    [Buccaneers and pirates of our coasts]
    Buccaneers and pirates / Frank R. Stockton ; with illustrations by George Varian and B. West Clinedinst. — Dover ed.
        p. cm.
    ISBN 0-486-45425-8
    1. Pirates—Juvenile literature. 2. Buccaneers—Juvenile literature. I. Title.

F2161.S86 2007
910.4'5—dc22

2007000141

Manufactured in the United States of America
Dover Publications, Inc., 31 East 2nd Street, Mineola, N.Y. 11501

# Contents

# Contents

# List of Illustrations

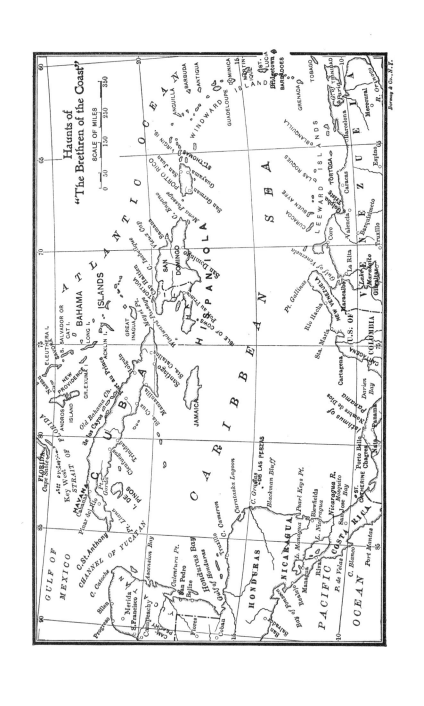

Haunts of
"The Brethren of the Coast"

SCALE OF MILES
0   50   150   250   350

Bormay & Co., N.Y.

# Buccaneers and Pirates

## Chapter I

### The Bold Buccaneers

WHEN I was a boy I strongly desired to be a pirate, and the reason for this was the absolute independence of that sort of life. Restrictions of all sorts had become onerous to me, and in my reading of the adventures of the bold sea-rovers of the main, I had unconsciously selected those portions of a pirate's life which were attractive to me, and had totally disregarded all the rest.

In fact, I had a great desire to become what might be called a marine Robin Hood. I would take from the rich and give to the poor; I would run my long, low, black craft by the side of the merchantman, and when I had loaded my vessel with the rich stuffs and golden ingots which composed her cargo, I would sail away to some poor village, and make its inhabitants prosperous and happy for

the rest of their lives by a judicious distribution of
my booty.

I would always be as free as a sea-bird.  My
men would be devoted to me, and my word would
be their law.  I would decide for myself whether
this or that proceeding would be proper, generous,
and worthy of my unlimited power; when tired
of sailing, I would retire to my island, — the position of which, in a beautiful semi-tropic ocean, would
be known only to myself and to my crew, — and
there I would pass happy days in the company of
my books, my works of art, and all the various
treasures I had taken from the mercenary vessels
which I had overhauled.

Such was my notion of a pirate's life.  I would
kill nobody; the very sight of my black flag
would be sufficient to put an end to all thought of
resistance on the part of my victims, who would
no more think of fighting me, than a fat bishop
would have thought of lifting his hand against
Robin Hood and his merry men; and I truly
believe that I expected my conscience to have a
great deal more to do in the way of approval of
my actions, than it had found necessary in the
course of my ordinary school-boy life.

I mention these early impressions because I have
a notion that a great many people — and not only
young people — have an idea of piracy not alto-

gether different from that of my boyhood. They
know that pirates are wicked men, that, in fact,
they are sea-robbers or maritime murderers, but
their bold and adventurous method of life, their
bravery, daring, and the exciting character of their
expeditions, give them something of the same charm
and interest which belong to the robber knights of
the middle ages. The one mounts his mailed steed
and clanks his long sword against his iron stirrup,
riding forth into the world with a feeling that he can
do anything that pleases him, if he finds himself
strong enough. The other springs into his rakish
craft, spreads his sails to the wind, and dashes over
the sparkling main with a feeling that he can do
anything he pleases, provided he be strong enough.

The first pirates who made themselves known in
American waters were the famous buccaneers; these
began their career in a very commonplace and un-
objectionable manner, and the name by which they
were known had originally no piratical significance.
It was derived from the French word *boucanier*,
signifying "a drier of beef."

Some of the West India islands, especially San
Domingo, were almost overrun with wild cattle of
various kinds, and this was owing to the fact that
the Spaniards had killed off nearly all the natives,
and so had left the interior of the islands to the
herds of cattle which had increased rapidly. There

were a few settlements on the seacoast, but the
Spaniards did not allow the inhabitants of these to
trade with any nation but their own, and consequently the people were badly supplied with the
necessaries of life.

But the trading vessels which sailed from Europe
to that part of the Caribbean Sea were manned by
bold and daring sailors, and when they knew that
San Domingo contained an abundance of beef cattle,
they did not hesitate to stop at the little seaports to
replenish their stores. The natives of the island
were skilled in the art of preparing beef by smoking
and drying it, — very much in the same way in
which our Indians prepare "jerked meat" for
winter use.

But so many vessels came to San Domingo for
beef that there were not enough people on the
island to do all the hunting and drying that was
necessary, so these trading vessels frequently anchored in some quiet cove, and the crews went on
shore and devoted themselves to securing a cargo
of beef, — not only enough for their own use, but
for trading purposes; thus they became known as
"beef-driers," or buccaneers.

When the Spaniards heard of this new industry
which had arisen within the limits of their possessions, they pursued the vessels of the buccaneers
wherever they were seen, and relentlessly destroyed

them and their crews. But there were not enough
Spanish vessels to put down the trade in dried beef;
more European vessels — generally English and
French — stopped at San Domingo; more bands
of hunting sailors made their way into the interior.
When these daring fellows knew that the Spaniards
were determined to break up their trade, they became more determined that it should not be broken
up, and they armed themselves and their vessels so
that they might be able to make a defence against
the Spanish men-of-war.

Thus gradually and almost imperceptibly a state
of maritime warfare grew up in the waters of the
West Indies between Spain and the beef-traders of
other nations; and from being obliged to fight, the
buccaneers became glad to fight, provided that it
was Spain they fought. True to her policy of
despotism and cruelty when dealing with her American possessions, Spain waged a bitter and bloody
war against the buccaneers who dared to interfere
with the commercial relations between herself and
her West India colonies, and in return, the buccaneers were just as bitter and savage in their warfare
against Spain. From defending themselves against
Spanish attacks, they began to attack Spaniards
whenever there was any chance of success, at first
only upon the sea, but afterwards on land. The
cruelty and ferocity of Spanish rule had brought

them into existence, and it was against Spain and her possessions that the cruelty and ferocity which she had taught them were now directed.

When the buccaneers had begun to understand each other and to effect organizations among themselves, they adopted a general name, — "The Brethren of the Coast." The outside world, especially the Spanish world, called them pirates, sea-robbers, buccaneers, — any title which would express their lawless character, but in their own denomination of themselves they expressed only their fraternal relations ; and for the greater part of their career, they truly stood by each other like brothers.

# Chapter II

## Some Masters in Piracy

FROM the very earliest days of history there have been pirates, and it is, therefore, not at all remarkable that, in the early days of the history of this continent, sea-robbers should have made themselves prominent; but the buccaneers of America differed in many ways from those pirates with whom the history of the old world has made us acquainted.

It was very seldom that an armed vessel set out from an European port for the express purpose of sea-robbery in American waters. At first nearly all the noted buccaneers were traders. But the circumstances which surrounded them in the new world made of them pirates whose evil deeds have never been surpassed in any part of the globe.

These unusual circumstances and amazing temptations do not furnish an excuse for the exceptionally wicked careers of the early American pirates; but we are bound to remember these causes or we could not understand the records of the settlement of the

West Indies. The buccaneers were fierce and reckless fellows who pursued their daring occupation because it was profitable, because they had learned to like it, and because it enabled them to wreak a certain amount of vengeance upon the common enemy. But we must not assume that they inaugurated the piratical conquests and warfare which existed so long upon our eastern seacoasts.

Before the buccaneers began their careers, there had been great masters of piracy who had opened their schools in the Caribbean Sea; and in order that the condition of affairs in this country during parts of the sixteenth and seventeenth centuries may be clearly understood, we will consider some of the very earliest noted pirates of the West Indies.

When we begin a judicial inquiry into the condition of our fellow-beings, we should try to be as courteous as we can, but we must be just; consequently a man's fame and position must not turn us aside, when we are acting as historical investigators.

Therefore, we shall be bold and speak the truth, and although we shall take off our hats and bow very respectfully, we must still assert that Christopher Columbus was the first who practised piracy in American waters.

When he sailed with his three little ships to discover unknown lands, he was an accredited explorer for the court of Spain, and was bravely sailing forth with an honest purpose, and with the same regard for law and justice as is possessed by any explorer of the present day. But when he discovered some unknown lands, rich in treasure and outside of all legal restrictions, the views and ideas of the great discoverer gradually changed. Being now beyond the boundaries of civilization, he also placed himself beyond the boundaries of civilized law. Robbery, murder, and the destruction of property, by the commanders of naval expeditions, who have no warrant or commission for their conduct, is the same as piracy, and when Columbus ceased to be a legalized explorer, and when, against the expressed wishes, and even the prohibitions, of the royal personages who had sent him out on this expedition, he began to devastate the countries he had discovered, and to enslave and exterminate their peaceable natives, then he became a master in piracy, from whom the buccaneers afterward learned many a valuable lesson.

It is not necessary for us to enter very deeply into the consideration of the policy of Columbus toward the people of the islands of the West Indies. His second voyage was nothing more than an expedition for the sake of plunder. He had discovered gold and other riches in the West Indies and he had found that the people who inhabited the islands were simple-hearted, inoffensive creatures, who did not know how to fight and who did not want to fight.

Therefore, it was so easy to sail his ships into the
harbors of defenceless islands, to subjugate the natives, and to take away the products of their mines
and soil, that he commenced a veritable course of
piracy.

The acquisition of gold and all sorts of plunder
seemed to be the sole object of this Spanish expedition; natives were enslaved, and subjected to
the greatest hardships, so that they died in great
numbers. At one time three hundred of them were
sent as slaves to Spain. A pack of bloodhounds,
which Columbus had brought with him for the purpose, was used to hunt down the poor Indians when
they endeavored to escape from the hands of the
oppressors, and in every way the island of Hayti,
the principal scene of the actions of Columbus, was
treated as if its inhabitants had committed a dreadful crime by being in possession of the wealth which
the Spaniards desired for themselves.

Queen Isabella was greatly opposed to these cruel
and unjust proceedings. She sent back to their
native land the slaves which Columbus had shipped
to Spain, and she gave positive orders that no more
of the inhabitants were to be enslaved, and that they
were all to be treated with moderation and kindness.
But the Atlantic is a wide ocean, and Columbus, far
away from his royal patron, paid little attention to
her wishes and commands; without going further

into the history of this period, we will simply mention the fact that it was on account of his alleged atrocities that Columbus was superseded in his command, and sent back in chains to Spain.

There was another noted personage of the sixteenth century who played the part of pirate in the new world, and thereby set a most shining example to the buccaneers of those regions. This was no other than Sir Francis Drake, one of England's greatest naval commanders.

It is probable that Drake, when he started out in life, was a man of very law-abiding and orderly disposition, for he was appointed by Queen Elizabeth a naval chaplain, and, it is said, though there is some doubt about this, that he was subsequently vicar of a parish. But by nature he was a sailor, and nothing else, and after having made several voyages in which he showed himself a good fighter, as well as a good commander, he undertook, in 1572, an expedition against the Spanish settlements in the West Indies, for which he had no legal warrant whatever.

Spain was not at war with England, and when Drake sailed with four small ships into the port of the little town of Nombre de Dios in the middle of the night, the inhabitants of the town were as much astonished as the people of Perth Amboy would be if four armed vessels were to steam into Raritan Bay, and endeavor to take possession of the

town. The peaceful Spanish townspeople were not
at war with any civilized nation, and they could not
understand why bands of armed men should invade
their streets, enter the market-place, fire their cali-
vers, or muskets, into the air, and then sound a
trumpet loud enough to wake up everybody in the
place. Just outside of the town the invaders had
left a portion of their men, and when these heard
the trumpet in the market-place, they also fired their
guns; all this noise and hubbub so frightened the
good people of the town, that many of them jumped
from their beds, and without stopping to dress, fled
away to the mountains. But all the citizens were
not such cowards, and fourteen or fifteen of them
armed themselves and went out to defend their town
from the unknown invaders.

Beginners in any trade or profession, whether it
be the playing of the piano, the painting of pictures,
or the pursuit of piracy, are often timid and dis-
trustful of themselves; so it happened on this occasion with Francis Drake and his men, who were
merely amateur pirates, and showed very plainly
that they did not yet understand their business.

When the fifteen Spanish citizens came into the
market-place and found there the little body of
armed Englishmen, they immediately fired upon
them, not knowing or caring who they were. This
brave resistance seems to have frightened Drake

and his men almost as much as their trumpets and guns had frightened the citizens, and the English immediately retreated from the town. When they reached the place where they had left the rest of their party, they found that these had already run away, and taken to the boats. Consequently Drake and his brave men were obliged to take off some of their clothes and to wade out to the little ships. The Englishmen secured no booty whatever, and killed only one Spaniard, who was a man who had been looking out of a window to see what was the matter.

Whether or not Drake's conscience had anything to do with the bungling manner in which he made this first attempt at piracy, we cannot say, but he soon gave his conscience a holiday, and undertook some very successful robbing enterprises. He received information from some natives, that a train of mules was coming across the Isthmus of Panama loaded with gold and silver bullion, and guarded only by their drivers ; for the merchants who owned all this treasure had no idea that there was any one in that part of the world who would commit a robbery upon them. But Drake and his men soon proved that they could hold up a train of mules as easily as some of the masked robbers in our western country hold up a train of cars. All the gold was taken, but the silver was too heavy for the amateur pirates to carry.

Two days after that, Drake and his men came to a place called " The House of Crosses," where they killed five or six peaceable merchants, but were greatly disappointed to find no gold, although the house was full of rich merchandise of various kinds. As his men had no means of carrying away heavy goods, he burned up the house and all its contents and went to his ships, and sailed away with the treasure he had already obtained.

Whatever this gallant ex-chaplain now thought of himself, he was considered by the Spaniards as an out-and-out pirate, and in this opinion they were quite correct. During his great voyage around the world, which he began in 1577, he came down upon the Spanish-American settlements like a storm from the sea. He attacked towns, carried off treasure, captured merchant-vessels, — and in fact showed himself to be a thoroughbred and accomplished pirate of the first class.

It was in consequence of the rich plunder with which his ships were now loaded, that he made his voyage around the world. He was afraid to go back the way he came, for fear of capture, and so, having passed the Straits of Magellan, and having failed to find a way out of the Pacific in the neighborhood of California, he doubled the Cape of Good Hope, and sailed along the western coast of Africa to European waters.

This grand piratical expedition excited great indignation in Spain, which country was still at peace with England, and even in England there were influential people who counselled the Queen that it would be wise and prudent to disavow Drake's actions, and compel him to restore to Spain the booty he had taken from his subjects. But Queen Elizabeth was not the woman to do that sort of thing. She liked brave men and brave deeds, and she was proud of Drake. Therefore, instead of punishing him, she honored him, and went to take dinner with him on board his ship, which lay at Deptford.

So Columbus does not stand alone as a grand master of piracy. The famous Sir Francis Drake, who became vice-admiral of the fleet which defeated the Spanish Armada, was a worthy companion of the great Genoese.

These notable instances have been mentioned because it would be unjust to take up the history of those resolute traders who sailed from England, France, and Holland, to the distant waters of the western world for the purpose of legitimate enterprise and commerce, and who afterwards became thorough-going pirates, without trying to make it clear that they had shining examples for their notable careers.

# Chapter III

## Pupils in Piracy

AFTER the discoveries of Columbus, the Spanish mind seems to have been filled with the idea that the whole undiscovered world, wherever it might be, belonged to Spain, and that no other nation had any right whatever to discover anything on the other side of the Atlantic, or to make any use whatever of lands which had been discovered. In fact, the natives of the new countries, and the inhabitants of all old countries except her own, were considered by Spain as possessing no rights whatever. If the natives refused to pay tribute, or to spend their days toiling for gold for their masters, or if vessels from England or France touched at one of their settlements for purposes of trade, it was all the same to the Spaniards; a war of attempted extermination was waged alike against the peaceful inhabitants of Hispaniola, now Hayti, and upon the bearded and hardy seamen from Northern Europe. Under this treatment the natives weakened and gradually disappeared;

but the buccaneers became more and more numerous and powerful.

The buccaneers were not unlike that class of men known in our western country as cowboys. Young fellows of good families from England and France often determined to embrace a life of adventure, and possibly profit, and sailed out to the West Indies to get gold and hides, and to fight Spaniards. Frequently they dropped their family names and assumed others more suitable to roving freebooters, and, like the bold young fellows who ride over our western plains, driving cattle and shooting Indians, they adopted a style of dress as free and easy, but probably not quite so picturesque, as that of the cowboy. They soon became a very rough set of fellows, in appearance as well as action, endeavoring in every way to let the people of the western world understand that they were absolutely free and independent of the manners and customs, as well as of the laws of their native countries.

So well was this independence understood, that when the buccaneers became strong enough to inflict some serious injury upon the settlements in the West Indies, and the Spanish court remonstrated with Queen Elizabeth on account of what had been done by some of her subjects, she replied that she had nothing to do with these buccaneers, who, although they had been born in England, had ceased for the time to be her subjects, and the Spaniards must defend themselves against them just as if they were an independent nation.

But it is impossible for men who have been brought up in civilized society, and who have been accustomed to obey laws, to rid themselves entirely of all ideas of propriety and morality, as soon as they begin a life of lawlessness. So it happened that many of the buccaneers could not divest themselves of the notions of good behavior to which they had been accustomed from youth. For instance, we are told of a captain of buccaneers, who, landing at a settlement on a Sunday, took his crew to church. As it is not at all probable that any of the buccaneering vessels carried chaplains, opportunities of attending services must have been rare. This captain seems to have wished to show that pirates in church know what they ought to do just as well as other people; it was for this reason that, when one of his men behaved himself in an improper and disorderly manner during the service, this proper-minded captain arose from his seat and shot the offender dead.

There was a Frenchman of that period who must have been a warm-hearted philanthropist, because, having read accounts of the terrible atrocities of the Spaniards in the western lands, he determined to leave his home and his family, and become a buccaneer, in order that he might do what he could for

the suffering natives in the Spanish possessions.
He entered into the great work which he had
planned for himself with such enthusiasm and zeal,
that in the course of time he came to be known as
" The Exterminator," and if there had been more
people of his philanthropic turn of mind, there
would soon have been no inhabitants whatever upon
the islands from which the Spaniards had driven
out the Indians.

There was another person of that day, — also a
Frenchman,—who became deeply involved in debt
in his own country, and feeling that the principles of
honor forbade him to live upon and enjoy what was
really the property of others, he made up his mind
to sail across the Atlantic, and become a buccaneer.
He hoped that if he should be successful in his new
profession, and should be enabled to rob Spaniards
for a term of years, he could return to France, pay
off all his debts, and afterward live the life of a man
of honor and respectability.

Other ideas which the buccaneers brought with
them from their native countries soon showed themselves when these daring sailors began their lives as
regular pirates ; among these, the idea of organization was very prominent.  Of course it was hard to
get a number of free and untrammelled crews to
unite and obey the commands of a few officers.
But in time the buccaneers had recognized leaders,

and laws were made for concerted action. In consequence of this the buccaneers became a formidable body of men, sometimes superior to the Spanish naval and military forces.

It must be remembered that the buccaneers lived in a very peculiar age. So far as the history of America is concerned, it might be called the age of blood and gold. In the newly discovered countries there were no laws which European nations or individuals cared to observe. In the West Indies and the adjacent mainlands there were gold and silver, and there were also valuable products of other kinds, and when the Spaniards sailed to their part of the new world, these treasures were the things for which they came. The natives were weak and not able to defend themselves. All the Spaniards had to do was to take what they could find, and when they could not find enough they made the poor Indians find it for them. Here was a part of the world, and an age of the world, wherein it was the custom for men to do what they pleased, provided they felt themselves strong enough, and it was not to be supposed that any one European nation could expect a monopoly of this state of mind.

Therefore it was that while the Spaniards robbed and ruined the natives of the lands they discovered, the English, French, and Dutch buccaneers robbed the robbers. Great vessels were sent out from

Spain, carrying nothing in the way of merchandise
to America, but returning with all the precious metals and valuable products of the newly discovered
regions, which could in any way be taken from the
unfortunate natives. The gold mines of the new
world had long been worked, and yielded handsome revenues, but the native method of operating
them did not satisfy the Spaniards, who forced the
poor Indians to labor incessantly at the difficult task
of digging out the precious metals, until many of
them died under the cruel oppression. Sometimes
the Indians were kept six months under ground,
working in the mines; and at one time, when it
was found that the natives had died off, or had fled
from the neighborhood of some of the rich gold
deposits, it was proposed to send to Africa and get
a cargo of negroes to work the mines.

Now it is easy to see that all this made buccaneering a very tempting occupation. To capture a
great treasure ship, after the Spaniards had been at
so much trouble to load it, was a grand thing,
according to the pirate's point of view, and although
it often required reckless bravery and almost super-
human energy to accomplish the feats necessary in
this dangerous vocation, these were qualities which
were possessed by nearly all the sea-robbers of
our coast; the stories of some of the most interesting of these wild and desperate fellows,—

men who did not combine piracy with discoveries and explorations, but who were out-and-out sea-robbers, and gained in that way all the reputation they ever possessed, — will be told in subsequent chapters.

## Chapter IV

### Peter the Great

VERY prominent among the early regular buccaneers was a Frenchman who came to be called Peter the Great. This man seems to have been one of those adventurers who were not buccaneers in the earlier sense of the word (by which I mean they were not traders who touched at Spanish settlements to procure cattle and hides, and who were prepared to fight any Spaniards who might interfere with them), but they were men who came from Europe on purpose to prey upon Spanish possessions, whether on land or sea. Some of them made a rough sort of settlement on the island of Tortuga, and then it was that Peter the Great seems to have come into prominence. He gathered about him a body of adherents, but although he had a great reputation as an individual pirate, it seems to have been a good while before he achieved any success as a leader.

The fortunes of Peter and his men must have

been at a pretty low ebb when they found' themselves cruising in a large, canoe-shaped boat not far
from the island of Hispaniola.    There were twenty-
nine of them in all, and they were not able to procure a vessel suitable for their purpose.    They
had been a long time floating about in an aimless
way, hoping to see some Spanish merchant-vessel
which they might attack and possibly capture, but
no such vessel appeared.    Their provisions began
to give out, the men were hungry, discontented, and
grumbling.    In fact, they were in almost as bad a
condition as were the sailors of Columbus just before they discovered signs of land, after their long
and weary voyage across the Atlantic.

When Peter and his men were almost on the
point of despair, they perceived, far away upon the
still waters, a large ship.    With a great jump, hope
sprang up in the breast of every man.    They seized
the oars and pulled in the direction of the distant
craft.    But when they were near enough, they saw
that the vessel was not a merchantman, probably
piled with gold and treasure, but a man-of-war
belonging to the Spanish fleet.    In fact, it was the
vessel of the vice-admiral.    This was an astonishing
and disheartening state of things.    It was very
much as if a lion, hearing the approach of probable
prey, had sprung from the thicket where he had
been concealed, and had beheld before him, not a

fine, fat deer, but an immense and scrawny elephant.

But the twenty-nine buccaneers in the crew were very hungry. They had not come out upon those waters to attack men-of-war, but, more than that, they had not come out to perish by hunger and thirst. There could be no doubt that there was plenty to eat and to drink on that tall Spanish vessel, and if they could not get food and water they could not live more than a day or two longer.

Under the circumstances it was not long before Peter the Great made up his mind that if his men would stand by him, he would endeavor to capture that Spanish war-vessel; when he put the question to his crew they all swore that they would follow him and obey his orders as long as life was left in their bodies. To attack a vessel armed with cannon, and manned by a crew very much larger than their little party, seemed almost like throwing themselves upon certain death. But still, there was a chance that in some way they might get the better of the Spaniards; whereas, if they rowed away again into the solitudes of the ocean, they would give up all chance of saving themselves from death by starvation. Steadily, therefore, they pulled toward the Spanish vessel, and slowly — for there was but little wind — she approached them.

The people in the man-of-war did not fail to per-

ceive the little boat far out on the ocean, and some
of them sent to the captain and reported the fact.
The news, however, did not interest him, for he
was engaged in playing cards in his cabin, and it was
not until an hour afterward that he consented to
come on deck and look out toward the boat which
had been sighted, and which was now much
nearer.

Taking a good look at the boat, and perceiving
that it was nothing more than a canoe, the captain
laughed at the advice of some of his officers, who
thought it would be well to fire a few cannon-shot
and sink the little craft. The captain thought it
would be a useless proceeding. He did not know
anything about the people in the boat, and he did
not very much care, but he remarked that if they
should come near enough, it might be a good thing
to put out some tackle and haul them and their
boat on deck, after which they might be examined
and questioned whenever it should suit his conven-
ience. Then he went down to his cards.

If Peter the Great and his men could have been
sure that if they were to row alongside the Spanish
vessel they would have been quietly hauled on deck
and examined, they would have been delighted at
the opportunity. With cutlasses, pistols, and knives,
they were more than ready to demonstrate to the
Spaniards what sort of fellows they were, and the

captain would have found hungry pirates uncomfortable persons to question.

But it seemed to Peter and his crew a very difficult thing indeed to get themselves on board the man-of-war, so they curbed their ardor and enthusiasm, and waited until nightfall before approaching nearer. As soon as it became dark enough they slowly and quietly paddled toward the great ship, which was now almost becalmed. There were no lights in the boat, and the people on the deck of the vessel saw and heard nothing on the dark waters around them.

When they were very near the man-of-war, the captain of the buccaneers — according to the ancient accounts of this adventure — ordered his chirurgeon, or surgeon, to bore a large hole in the bottom of their canoe. It is probable that this officer, with his saws and other surgical instruments, was expected to do carpenter work when there were no duties for him to perform in the regular line of his profession. At any rate, he went to work, and noiselessly bored the hole.

This remarkable proceeding showed the desperate character of these pirates. A great, almost impossible task was before them, and nothing but absolute recklessness could enable them to succeed. If his men should meet with strong opposition from the Spaniards in the proposed attack, and if any of them should become frightened and try to retreat to the boat, Peter knew that all would be lost, and consequently he determined to make it impossible for any man to get away in that boat. If they could not conquer the Spanish vessel they must die on her decks.

When the half-sunken canoe touched the sides of the vessel, the pirates, seizing every rope or projection on which they could lay their hands, climbed up the sides of the man-of-war, as if they had been twenty-nine cats, and springing over the rail, dashed upon the sailors who were on' deck. These men were utterly stupefied and astounded. They had seen nothing, they had heard nothing, and all of a sudden they were confronted with savage fellows with cutlasses and pistols.

Some of the crew looked over the sides to see where these strange visitors had come from, but they saw nothing, for the canoe had gone to the bottom. Then they were filled with a superstitious horror, believing that the wild visitors were devils who had dropped from the sky, for there seemed no other place from which they could come. Making no attempt to defend themselves, the sailors, wild with terror, tumbled below and hid themselves, without even giving an alarm.

The Spanish captain was still playing cards, and whether he was winning or losing, the old historians do not tell us, but very suddenly a newcomer took a hand in the game. This was Peter the Great, and he played the ace of trumps. With a great pistol in his hand, he called upon the Spanish captain to surrender. That noble commander glanced around. There was a savage pirate holding a pistol at the head of each of the officers at the table. He threw up his cards. The trick was won by Peter and his men.

The rest of the game was easy enough. When the pirates spread themselves over the vessel, the frightened crew got out of sight as well as they could. Some, who attempted to seize their arms in order to defend themselves, were ruthlessly cut down or shot, and when the hatches had been securely fastened upon the sailors who had fled below, Peter the Great was captain and owner of that tall Spanish man-of-war.

It is quite certain that the first thing these pirates did to celebrate their victory was to eat a rousing good supper, and then they took charge of the vessel, and sailed her triumphantly over the waters on which, not many hours before, they had feared that a little boat would soon be floating, filled with their emaciated bodies.

This most remarkable success of Peter the Great worked a great change, of course, in the circumstances of himself and his men. But it worked

a greater change in the career, and possibly in the
character of the captain.   He was now a very rich
man, and all his followers had plenty of money.
The Spanish vessel was amply supplied with provisions, and there was also on board a great quantity of gold bullion, which was to be shipped to
Spain.   In fact, Peter and his men had booty
enough to satisfy any sensible pirate.   Now we all
know that sensible pirates, and people in any sphere
of life who are satisfied when they have enough, are
very rare indeed, and therefore it is not a little surprising that the bold buccaneer, whose story we are
now telling, should have proved that he merited, in
a certain way, the title his companions had given
him.

Sailing his prize to the shores of Hispaniola,
Peter put on shore all the Spaniards whose services
he did not desire.   The rest of his prisoners he
compelled to help his men work the ship, and then,
without delay, he sailed away to France, and there
he retired entirely from the business of piracy, and
set himself up as a gentleman of wealth and leisure.

# Chapter V

## The Story of a Pearl Pirate

THE ordinary story of the pirate, or the wicked man in general, no matter how successful he may have been in his criminal career, nearly always ends disastrously, and in that way points a moral which doubtless has a good effect on a large class of people, who would be very glad to do wrong, provided no harm was likely to come to them in consequence. But the story of Peter the Great, which we have just told, contains no such moral. In fact, its influence upon the adventurers of that period was most unwholesome.

When the wonderful success of Peter the Great became known, the buccaneering community at Tortuga was wildly excited. Every bushy-bearded fellow who could get possession of a small boat, and induce a score of other bushy-bearded fellows to follow him, wanted to start out and capture a rich Spanish galleon, as the great ships, used alike for war and commerce, were then called.

But not only were the French and English sailors

and traders who had become buccaneers excited and
stimulated by the remarkable good fortune of their
companion, but many people of adventurous mind,
who had never thought of leaving England for purposes of piracy, now became firmly convinced that
there was no business which promised better than
that of a buccaneer, and some of them crossed the
ocean for the express purpose of getting rich by
capturing Spanish vessels homeward bound.

As there were not enough suitable vessels in Tortuga for the demands of the recently stimulated
industry, the buccaneer settlers went to other parts
of the West Indies to obtain suitable craft, and it is
related that in about a month after the great victory
of Peter the Great, two large Spanish vessels, loaded
with silver bullion, and two other heavily laden merchantmen were brought into Tortuga by the buccaneers.

One of the adventurers who set out about this
time on a cruise after gold-laden vessels, was a
Frenchman who was known to his countrymen as
Pierre François, and to the English as Peter Francis.
He was a good sailor, and ready for any sort of a
sea-fight, but for a long time he cruised about without seeing anything which it was worth while to
attempt to capture. At last, when his provisions
began to give out, and his men became somewhat
discontented, Pierre made up his mind that rather

than return to Tortuga empty-handed, he would make a bold and novel stroke for fortune.

At the mouth of one of the large rivers of the mainland the Spaniards had established a pearl fishery, — for there was no kind of wealth or treasure, on the land, under ground, or at the bottom of the sea, that the Spaniards did not get if it were possible for them to do so.

Every year, at the proper season, a dozen or more vessels came to this pearl-bank, attended by a man-of-war to protect them from molestation. Pierre knew all about this, and as he could not find any Spanish merchantmen to rob, he thought he would go down and see what he could do with the pearl-fishers. This was something the buccaneers had not yet attempted, but no one knows what he can do until he tries, and it was very necessary that this buccaneer captain should try something immediately.

When he reached the coast near the mouth of the river, he took the masts out of his little vessel, and rowed quietly toward the pearl-fishing fleet, as if he had intended to join them on some entirely peaceable errand; and, in fact, there was no reason whatever why the Spaniards should suppose that a boat full of buccaneers should be rowing along that part of the coast.

The pearl-fishing vessels were all at anchor, and the people on board were quietly attending to their

business. Out at sea, some distance from the mouth
of the river, the man-of-war was lying becalmed.
The native divers who went down to the bottom
of the sea to bring up the shellfish which contained
the pearls, plunged into the water, and came up wet
and shining in the sun, with no fear whatever of any
sharks which might be swimming about in search of
a dinner, and the people on the vessels opened the
oysters and carefully searched for pearls, feeling as
safe from harm as if they were picking olives in their
native groves.

But something worse than a shark was quietly
making its way over those tranquil waters, and no
banditti who ever descended from Spanish mountains upon the quiet peasants of a village, equalled
in ferocity the savage fellows who were crouching in
the little boat belonging to Pierre of Tortuga.

This innocent-looking craft, which the pearl-
fishers probably thought was loaded with fruit or
vegetables which somebody from the mainland
desired to sell, was permitted, without being challenged or interfered with, to row up alongside the
largest vessel of the fleet, on which there were some
armed men and a few cannon.

As soon as Pierre's boat touched the Spanish
vessel, the buccaneers sprang on board with their
pistols and cutlasses, and a savage fight began. The
Spaniards were surprised, but there were a great

many more of them than there were pirates, and
they fought hard. However, the man who makes
the attack, and who is at the same time desperate
and hungry, has a great advantage, and it was not
long before the buccaneers were masters of the
vessel. Those of the Spaniards who were not
killed, were forced into the service of their captors,
and Pierre found himself in command of a very
good vessel.

Now it so happened that the man-of-war was so
far away that she knew nothing of this fight on board
one of the fleet which she was there to watch, and
if she had known of it, she would not have been
able to give any assistance, for there was no wind
by which she could sail to the mouth of the river.
Therefore, so far as she was concerned, Pierre considered himself safe.

But although he had captured a Spanish ship, he
was not so foolish as to haul down her flag, and run
up his own in her place. He had had very good
success so far, but he was not satisfied. It was
quite probable that there was a rich store of pearls
on board the vessel he had taken, but on the other
vessels of the fleet there were many more pearls,
and these he wanted if he could get them. In fact,
he conceived the grand idea of capturing the whole
fleet.

But it would be impossible for Pierre to attempt

anything on such a magnificent scale until he had first disposed of the man-of-war, and as he had now a good strong ship, with a much larger crew than that with which he had set out, — for the Spanish prisoners would be obliged to man the guns and help in every way to fight their countrymen, — Pierre determined to attack the man-of-war.

A land wind began to blow, which enabled him to make very fair headway out to sea. The Spanish colors were flying from his topmast, and he hoped to be able, without being suspected of any evil designs, to get so near to the man-of-war that he might run alongside and boldly board her.

But something now happened which Pierre could not have expected. When the commander of the war-vessel perceived that one of the fleet under his charge was leaving her companions and putting out to sea, he could imagine no reason for such extraordinary conduct, except that she was taking advantage of the fact that the wind had not yet reached his vessel, and was trying to run away with the pearls she had on board. From these ready suspicions we may imagine that, at that time, the robbers who robbed robbers were not all buccaneers.

Soon after the Spanish captain perceived that one of his fleet was making his way out of the river, the wind reached his vessel, and he immediately set all

"They set all sail, and there was a fine sea-chase." — p. 37.

sail and started in pursuit of the rascals, whom he supposed to be his dishonest countrymen.

The breeze freshened rapidly, and when Pierre and his men saw that the man-of-war was coming toward them at a good rate of speed, showing plainly that she had suspicions of them, they gave up all hope of running alongside of her and boarding her, and concluded that the best thing they could do would be to give up their plan of capturing the pearl-fishing fleet, and get away with the ship they had taken, and whatever it had on board. So they set all sail, and there was a fine sea-chase.

The now frightened buccaneers were too anxious to get away. They not only put on all the sail which the vessel could carry, but they put on more. The wind blew harder, and suddenly down came the mainmast with a crash. This stopped the chase, and the next act in the performance would have to be a sea-fight. Pierre and his buccaneers were good at that sort of thing, and when the man-of-war came up, there was a terrible time on board those two vessels. But the Spaniards were the stronger, and the buccaneers were defeated.

There must have been something in the daring courage of this Frenchman and his little band of followers, which gave him favor in the eyes of the Spanish captain, for there was no other reason for the good treatment which the buccaneers received.

They were not put to the sword nor thrown
overboard, not sent on shore and made to work as
slaves, — three very common methods of treating
prisoners in those days. But they were all set free,
and put on land, where they might go where they
pleased.

This unfortunate result of the bold enterprise
undertaken by Pierre François was deeply deplored,
not only at Tortuga, but in England and in France.
If this bold buccaneer had captured the pearl fleet,
it would have been a victory that would have made
a hero of him on each side of the Atlantic, but had
he even been able to get away with the one vessel
he had seized, he would have been a rich man, and
might have retired to a life of ease and affluence;
the vessel he had captured proved to be one of the
richest laden of the whole fleet, and not only in
the heart of Pierre and his men, but among his
sympathizers in Europe and America, there was
great disappointment at the loss of that mainmast,
which, until it cracked, was carrying him forward to
fame and fortune.

# Chapter VI

## The Surprising Adventures of Bartholemy Portuguez

AS we have seen that the buccaneers were mainly English, French, and Dutch sailors, who were united to make a common piratical warfare upon the Spaniards in the West Indies, it may seem a little strange to find a man from Portugal who seemed to be on the wrong side of this peculiar fight which was going on in the new world between the sailors of Northern and Southern Europe. But although Portugal is such a close neighbor of Spain, the two countries have often been at war with each other, and their interests are by no means the same. The only advantage that Portugal could expect from the newly discovered treasures of the West were those which her seafaring men, acting with the seafaring men of other nations, should wrest from Spanish vessels homeward bound.

Consequently, there were Portuguese among the pirates of those days. Among these was a man named Bartholemy Portuguez, a famous *flibustier*.

It may be here remarked that the name of buccanneer was chiefly affected by the English adventurers
on our coast, while the French members of the profession often preferred the name of "flibustier." This
word, which has since been corrupted into our familiar "filibuster," is said to have been originally a corruption, being nothing more than the French method
of pronouncing the word "freebooters," which title
had long been used for independent robbers.

Thus, although Bartholemy called himself a flibustier, he was really a buccaneer, and his name came
to be known all over the Caribbean Sea. From
the accounts we have of him it appears that he did
not start out on his career of piracy as a poor man.
He had some capital to invest in the business, and
when he went over to the West Indies he took
with him a small ship, armed with four small cannon, and manned by a crew of picked men, many
of them no doubt professional robbers, and the
others anxious for practice in this most alluring
vocation, for the gold fields of California were
never more attractive to the bold and hardy adventurers of our country, than were the gold fields of
the sea to the buccaneers and flibustiers of the
seventeenth century.

When Bartholemy reached the Caribbean Sea he
probably first touched at Tortuga, the pirates' headquarters, and then sailed out very much as if he

had been a fisherman going forth to see what he
could catch on the sea.   He cruised about on
the track generally taken by treasure ships going
from the mainland to the Havanas, or the island
of Hispaniola, and when at last he sighted a vessel
in the distance, it was not long before he and his
men had made up their minds that if they were to
have any sport that day it would be with what
might be called most decidedly a game fish, for
the ship slowly sailing toward them was a large
Spanish vessel, and from her portholes there pro-
truded the muzzles of at least twenty cannon.   Of
course, they knew that such a vessel would have a
much larger crew than their own, and, altogether,
Bartholemy was very much in the position of a man
who should go out to harpoon a sturgeon, and who
should find himself confronted by a vicious sword-
fish.

The Spanish merchantmen of that day were generally well armed, for getting home safely across
the Atlantic was often the most difficult part of the
treasure-seeking.   There were many of these ships,
which, although they did not belong to the Spanish
navy, might almost be designated as men-of-war,
and it was one of these with which our flibustier
had now met.

But pirates and fishermen cannot afford to pick
and choose.   They must take what comes to them

and make the best of it, and this is exactly the way
in which the matter presented itself to Bartholemy
and his men. They held one of their councils
around the mast, and after an address from their
leader, they decided that come what may, they must
attack that Spanish vessel.

So the little pirate sailed boldly toward the big
Spaniard, and the latter vessel, utterly astonished
at the audacity of this attack, — for the pirates' flag
was flying, — lay to, head to the wind, and waited,
the gunners standing by their cannon. When the
pirates had come near enough to see and understand the size and power of the vessel they had
thought of attacking, they did not, as might have
been expected, put about and sail away at the best
of their vessel's speed, but they kept straight on
their course as if they had been about to fall upon
a great, unwieldy merchantman, manned by common sailors.

Perceiving the foolhardiness of the little vessel,
the Spanish commander determined to give it a lesson which would teach its captain to understand better the relative power of great vessels and little ones,
so, as soon as the pirates' vessel was near enough,
he ordered a broadside fired upon it. The Spanish
ship had a great many people on board. It had
a crew of seventy men, and besides these there were
some passengers, and regular marines, and knowing

that the captain had determined to fire upon the
approaching vessel, everybody had gathered on deck
to see the little pirate ship go down.

But the ten great cannon-balls which were shot
out at Bartholemy's little craft all missed their aim,
and before the guns could be reloaded or the great
ship be got around so as to deliver her other broadside, the pirate vessel was alongside of her. Bartholemy had fired none of his cannon. Such guns
were useless against so huge a foe. What he was
after was a hand-to-hand combat on the deck of the
Spanish ship.

The pirates were all ready for hot work. They
had thrown aside their coats and shirts as if each
of them were going into a prize fight, and, with their
cutlasses in their hands, and their pistols and knives
in their belts, they scrambled like monkeys up
the sides of the great ship. But Spaniards are
brave men and good fighters, and there were more
than twice as many of them as there were of the
pirates, and it was not long before the latter found
out that they could not capture that vessel by
boarding it. So over the side they tumbled as fast
as they could go, leaving some of their number
dead and wounded behind them. They jumped
into their own vessel, and then they put off to a
short distance to take breath and get ready for
a different kind of a fight. The triumphant Span-

iards now prepared to get rid of this boat load of
half-naked wild beasts, which they could easily do
if they should take better aim with their cannon
than they had done before.

But to their amazement they soon found that
they could do nothing with the guns, nor were they
able to work their ship so as to get it into position
for effectual shots. Bartholemy and his men laid
aside their cutlasses and their pistols, and took up
their muskets, with which they were well provided.
Their vessel lay within a very short range of the
Spanish ship, and whenever a man could be seen
through the portholes, or showed himself in the
rigging or anywhere else where it was necessary to
go in order to work the ship, he made himself
a target for the good aim of the pirates. The
pirate vessel could move about as it pleased, for it
required but a few men to manage it, and so it
kept out of the way of the Spanish guns, and its
best marksmen, crouching close to the deck, fired
and fired whenever a Spanish head was to be
seen.

For five long hours this unequal contest was kept
up. It might have reminded one of a man with a
slender rod and a long, delicate line, who had hooked
a big salmon. The man could not pull in the salmon, but, on the other hand, the salmon could not
hurt the man, and in the course of time the big fish

" The best marksmen, crouching close to the deck, fired and fired
whenever a Spanish head was to be seen." — p. 44.

would be tired out, and the man would get out his landing-net and scoop him in.

Now Bartholemy thought he could scoop in the Spanish vessel. So many of her men had been shot that the two crews would be more nearly equal. So, boldly, he ran his vessel alongside the big ship and again boarded her. Now there was another great fight on the decks. The Spaniards had ceased to be triumphant, but they had become desperate, and in the furious combat ten of the pirates were killed and four wounded. But the Spaniards fared worse than that; more than half of the men who had not been shot by the pirates went down before their cutlasses and pistols, and it was not long before Bartholemy had captured the great Spanish ship.

It was a fearful and a bloody victory he had gained. A great part of his own men were lying dead or helpless on the deck, and of the Spaniards only forty were left alive, and these, it appears from the accounts, must have been nearly all wounded or disabled.

It was a common habit among the buccaneers, as well as among the Spaniards, to kill all prisoners who were not able to work for them, but Bartholemy does not seem to have arrived at the stage of depravity necessary for this. So he determined not to kill his prisoners, but he put them all into a boat and let them go where they pleased; while he was left with fifteen men to work a great vessel which required a crew of five times that number.

But the men who could conquer and capture a ship against such enormous odds, felt themselves fully capable of working her, even with their little crew. Before doing anything in the way of navigation they cleared the decks of the dead bodies, taking from them all watches, trinkets, and money, and then went below to see what sort of a prize they had gained. They found it a very good one indeed. There were seventy-five thousand crowns in money, besides a cargo of cocoa worth five thousand more, and this, combined with the value of the ship and all its fittings, was a great fortune for those days.

When the victorious pirates had counted their gains and had mended the sails and rigging of their new ship, they took what they wanted out of their own vessel, and left her to sink or to float as she pleased, and then they sailed away in the direction of the island of Jamaica. But the winds did not suit them, and, as their crew was so very small, they could not take advantage of light breezes as they could have done if they had had men enough. Consequently they were obliged to stop to get water before they reached the friendly vicinity of Jamaica.

They cast anchor at Cape St. Anthony on the west end of Cuba. After a considerable delay at this place they started out again to resume their voyage, but it was not long before they perceived, to their horror, three Spanish vessels coming towards them. It was impossible for a very large ship, manned by an extremely small crew, to sail away from those fully equipped vessels, and as to attempting to defend themselves against the overwhelming power of the antagonists, that was too absurd to be thought of even by such a reckless fellow as Bartholemy. So, when the ship was hailed by the Spanish vessels he lay to and waited until a boat's crew boarded him. With the eye of a nautical man the Spanish captain of one of the ships perceived that something was the matter with this vessel, for its sails and rigging were terribly cut up in the long fight through which it had passed, and of course he wanted to know what had happened. When he found that the great ship was in the possession of a very small body of pirates, Bartholemy and his men were immediately made prisoners, taken on board the Spanish ship, stripped of everything they possessed, even their clothes, and shut up in the hold. A crew from the Spanish ships was sent to man the vessel which had been captured, and then the little fleet set sail for San Francisco in Campeachy.

An hour had worked a very great change in the fortunes of Bartholemy and his men; in the fine cabin of their grand prize they had feasted and sung, and had gloried over their wonderful success, and now, in the vessel of their captor, they were shut up in the dark, to be enslaved or perhaps executed.

But it is not likely that any one of them either despaired or repented; these are sentiments very little in use by pirates.

## Chapter VII

### The Pirate who could not Swim

WHEN the little fleet of Spanish vessels, including the one which had been captured by Bartholemy Portuguez and his men, were on their way to Campeachy, they met with very stormy weather so that they were separated, and the ship which contained Bartholemy and his companions arrived first at the port for which they were bound.

The captain, who had Bartholemy and the others in charge, did not know what an important capture he had made; he supposed that these pirates were ordinary buccaneers, and it appears that it was his intention to keep them as his own private prisoners, for, as they were all very able-bodied men, they would be extremely useful on a ship. But when his vessel was safely moored, and it became known in the town that he had a company of pirates on board, a great many people came from shore to see these savage men, who were probably looked upon

very much as if they were a menagerie of wild beasts
brought from foreign lands.

Among the sightseers who came to the ship was
a merchant of the town who had seen Bartholemy
before, and who had heard of his various exploits.
He therefore went to the captain of the vessel and
informed him that he had on board one of the very
worst pirates in the whole world, whose wicked
deeds were well known in various parts of the West
Indies, and who ought immediately to be delivered
up to the civil authorities. This proposal, however,
met with no favor from the Spanish captain, who
had found Bartholemy a very quiet man, and could
see that he was a very strong one, and he did not
at all desire to give up such a valuable addition to
his crew. But the merchant grew very angry, for
he knew that Bartholemy had inflicted great injury
on Spanish commerce, and as the captain would not
listen to him, he went to the Governor of the town
and reported the case. When this dignitary heard
the story he immediately sent a party of officers to
the ship, and commanded the captain to deliver the
pirate leader into their charge. The other men
were left where they were, but Bartholemy was
taken away and confined in another ship. The
merchant, who seemed to know a great deal about
him, informed the authorities that this terrible pirate
had been captured several times, but that he had

always managed to escape, and, therefore, he was
put in irons, and preparations were made to execute
him on the next day; for, from what he had heard,
the Governor considered that this pirate was no
better than a wild beast, and that he should be put
to death without even the formality of a trial.

But there was a Spanish soldier on board the ship
who seemed to have had some pity, or perhaps some
admiration, for the daring pirate, and he thought
that if he were to be hung the next day it was no
more than right to let him know it, so that when
he went in to take some food to Bartholemy he
told him what was to happen.

Now this pirate captain was a man who always
wanted to have a share in what was to happen, and
he immediately racked his brain to find out what
he could do in this case. He had never been in a
more desperate situation, but he did not lose heart,
and immediately set to work to free himself from
his irons, which were probably very clumsy affairs.
At last, caring little how much he scratched and tore
his skin, he succeeded in getting rid of his fetters,
and could move about as freely as a tiger in a
cage. To get out of this cage was Bartholemy's
first object. It would be comparatively easy, because in the course of time some one would come
into the hold, and the athletic buccaneer thought
that he could easily get the better of whoever might

open the hatch. But the next act in this truly
melodramatic performance would be a great deal
more difficult; for in order to escape from the ship
it would be absolutely necessary for Bartholemy to
swim to shore, and he did not know how to swim,
which seems a strange failing in a hardy sailor with
so many other nautical accomplishments. In the
rough hold where he was shut up, our pirate, peer-
ing about, anxious and earnest, discovered two large
earthen jars in which wine had been brought from
Spain, and with these he determined to make a sort
of life-preserver. He found some pieces of oiled
cloth, which he tied tightly over the open mouths
of the jars and fastened them with cords. He was
satisfied that this unwieldy contrivance would support him in the water.

Among other things he had found in his rum-
magings about the hold was an old knife, and with
this in his hand he now sat waiting for a good opportunity to attack his sentinel.

This came soon after nightfall. A man descended with a lantern to see that the prisoner
was still secure, — let us hope that it was not
the soldier who had kindly informed him of his
fate, — and as soon as he was fairly in the hold
Bartholemy sprang upon him. There was a fierce
struggle, but the pirate was quick and powerful,
and the sentinel was soon dead. Then, carrying

"The pirate soon floated out of sight and hearing." — p. 53.

his two jars, Bartholemy climbed swiftly and noise-lessly up the short ladder, came out on deck in the darkness, made a rush toward the side of the ship, and leaped overboard. For a moment he sank below the surface, but the two air-tight jars quickly rose and bore him up with them. There was a bustle on board the ship, there was some random firing of muskets in the direction of the splashing which the watch had heard, but none of the balls struck the pirate or his jars, and he soon floated out of sight and hearing. Kicking out with his legs, and paddling as well as he could with one hand while he held on to the jars with the other, he at last managed to reach the land, and ran as fast as he could into the dark woods beyond the town.

Bartholemy was now greatly in fear that, when his escape was discovered, he would be tracked by bloodhounds, — for these dogs were much used by the Spaniards in pursuing escaping slaves or prison-ers, — and he therefore did not feel safe in immedi-ately making his way along the coast, which was what he wished to do. If the hounds should get upon his trail, he was a lost man. The desperate pirate, therefore, determined to give the blood-hounds no chance to follow him, and for three days he remained in a marshy forest, in the dark recesses of which he could hide, and where the water, which covered the ground, prevented the dogs from following his scent. He had nothing to eat except a few roots of water-plants, but he was accustomed to privation, and these kept him alive. Often he heard the hounds baying on the dry land adjoining the marsh, and sometimes he saw at night distant torches, which he was sure were carried by men who were hunting for him.

But at last the pursuit seemed to be given up; and hearing no more dogs and seeing no more flickering lights, Bartholemy left the marsh and set out on his long journey down the coast. The place he wished to reach was called Golpho Triste, which was forty leagues away, but where he had reason to suppose he would find some friends. When he came out from among the trees, he mounted a small hill and looked back upon the town. The public square was lighted, and there in the middle of it he saw the gallows which had been erected for his execution, and this sight, doubtless, animated him very much during the first part of his journey.

The terrible trials and hardships which Bartholemy experienced during his tramp along the coast were such as could have been endured only by one of the strongest and toughest of men. He had found in the marsh an old gourd, or calabash, which he had filled with fresh water,—for he could

expect nothing but sea-water during his journey, —
and as for solid food he had nothing but the raw
shellfish which he found upon the rocks; but after
a diet of roots, shellfish must have been a very
agreeable change, and they gave him all the strength
and vigor he needed.  Very often he found streams
and inlets which he was obliged to ford, and as he
could see that they were always filled with alligators,
the passage of them was not very pleasant.  His
method of getting across one of these narrow streams,
was to hurl rocks into the water until he had frightened away the alligators immediately in front of
him, and then, when he had made for himself what
seemed to be a free passage, he would dash in and
hurry across.

At other times great forests stretched down to
the very coast, and through these he was obliged to
make his way, although he could hear the roars and
screams of wild beasts all about him.  Any one who
is afraid to go down into a dark cellar to get some
apples from a barrel at the foot of the stairs, can
have no idea of the sort of mind possessed by
Bartholemy Portuguez.  The animals might howl
around him and glare at him with their shining
eyes, and the alligators might lash the water into
foam with their great tails, but he was bound for
Golpho Triste and was not to be stopped on his
way by anything alive.

But at last he came to something not alive, which
seemed to be an obstacle which would certainly get
the better of him. This was a wide river, flowing
through the inland country into the sea. He
made his way up the shore of this river for a considerable distance, but it grew but little narrower,
and he could see no chance of getting across. He
could not swim and he had no wine-jars now with
which to buoy himself up, and if he had been able
to swim he would probably have been eaten up by
alligators soon after he left the shore. But a man
in his situation would not be likely to give up
readily; he had done so much that he was ready
to do more if he could only find out what to do.

Now a piece of good fortune happened to him,
although to an ordinary traveller it might have been
considered a matter of no importance whatever.
On the edge of the shore, where it had floated
down from some region higher up the river, Bartholemy perceived an old board, in which there
were some long and heavy rusty nails. Greatly
encouraged by this discovery the indefatigable
traveller set about a work which resembled that
of the old woman who wanted a needle, and who
began to rub a crow-bar on a stone in order to
reduce it to the proper size. Bartholemy carefully
knocked all the nails out of the board, and then
finding a large flat stone, he rubbed down one of

them until he had formed it into the shape of a
rude knife blade, which he made as sharp as he
could.    Then with these tools he undertook the
construction of a raft, working away like a beaver,
and using the sharpened nails instead of his teeth.
He cut down a number of small trees, and when he
had enough of these slender trunks he bound them
together with reeds and osiers, which he found on
the river bank.    So, after infinite labor and trial he
constructed a raft which would bear him on the
surface of the water.    When he had launched this
he got upon it, gathering up his legs so as to keep
out of reach of the alligators, and with a long pole
pushed himself off from shore.    Sometimes paddling
and sometimes pushing his pole against the bottom,
he at last got across the river and took up his journey upon dry land.

But our pirate had not progressed very far upon
the other side of the river before he met with a new
difficulty of a very formidable character.    This was
a great forest of mangrove trees, which grow in
muddy and watery places and which have many
roots, some coming down from the branches, and
some extending themselves in a hopeless tangle in
the water and mud.    It would have been impossible for even a stork to walk through this forest,
but as there was no way of getting around it Bartholemy determined to go through it, even if he

could not walk.   No athlete of the present day, no
matter if he should be a most accomplished circus-
man, could reasonably expect to perform the feat
which this bold pirate successfully accomplished.
For five or six leagues he went through that mangrove forest, never once setting his foot upon the
ground, — by which is meant mud, water, and roots,
— but swinging himself by his hands and arms,
from branch to branch, as if he had been a great ape,
only resting occasionally, drawing himself upon a
stout limb where he might sit for a while and get
his breath.   If he had slipped while he was swinging
from one limb to another and had gone down into
the mire and roots beneath him, it is likely that he
would never have been able to get out alive.   But
he made no slips.   He might not have had the
agility and grace of a trapeze performer, but his
grasp was powerful and his arms were strong, and
so he swung and clutched, and clutched and swung,
until he had gone entirely through the forest and
had come out on the open coast.

## Chapter VIII

### How Bartholemy rested Himself

IT was full two weeks from the time that Bartholemy began his most adventurous and difficult journey before he reached the little town of Golpho Triste, where, as he had hoped, he found some of his buccaneer friends. Now that his hardships and dangers were over, and when, instead of roots and shellfish, he could sit down to good, plentiful meals, and stretch himself upon a comfortable bed, it might have been supposed that Bartholemy would have given himself a long rest, but this hardy pirate had no desire for a vacation at this time. Instead of being worn out and exhausted by his amazing exertions and semi-starvation, he arrived among his friends vigorous and energetic and exceedingly anxious to recommence business as soon as possible. He told them of all that had happened to him, what wonderful good fortune had come to him, and what terrible bad fortune had quickly followed it, and when he had related his adventures and his dangers he astonished even his

piratical friends by asking them to furnish him with
a small vessel and about twenty men, in order that
he might go back and revenge himself, not only for
what had happened to him, but for what would
have happened if he had not taken his affairs into
his own hands.

To do daring and astounding deeds is part of the
business of a pirate, and although it was an uncom-
monly bold enterprise that Bartholemy contemplated, he got his vessel and he got his men, and
away he sailed. After a voyage of about eight days
he came in sight of the little seaport town, and sailing
slowly along the coast, he waited until nightfall
before entering the harbor. Anchored at a considerable distance from shore was the great Spanish
ship on which he had been a prisoner, and from
which he would have been taken and hung in the
public square; the sight of the vessel filled his soul
with a savage fury known only to pirates and bull
dogs.

As the little vessel slowly approached the great
ship, the people on board the latter thought it was a
trading-vessel from shore, and allowed it to come
alongside, such small craft seldom coming from the
sea. But the moment Bartholemy reached the ship
he scrambled up its side almost as rapidly as he had
jumped down from it with his two wine-jars a few
weeks before, and every one of his crew, leaving

their own vessel to take care of itself, scrambled up
after him.

Nobody on board was prepared to defend the
ship. It was the same old story; resting quietly in
a peaceful harbor, what danger had they to expect?
As usual the pirates had everything their own way;
they were ready to fight, and the others were not,
and they were led by a man who was determined to
take that ship without giving even a thought to
the ordinary alternative of dying in the attempt.
The affair was more of a massacre than a combat,
and there were people on board who did not know
what was taking place until the vessel had been
captured.

As soon as Bartholemy was master of the great
vessel he gave orders to slip the cable and hoist the
sails, for he was anxious to get out of that harbor
as quickly as possible. The fight had apparently
attracted no attention in the town, but there were
ships in the port whose company the bold buccaneer
did not at all desire, and as soon as possible he got
his grand prize under way and went sailing out of
the port.

Now, indeed, was Bartholemy triumphant; the
ship he had captured was a finer one and a richer
one than that other vessel which had been taken
from him. It was loaded with valuable merchandise, and we may here remark that for some reason

or other all Spanish vessels of that day which were
so unfortunate as to be taken by pirates, seemed to
be richly laden.

If our bold pirate had sung wild pirate songs, as
he passed the flowing bowl while carousing with his
crew in the cabin of the Spanish vessel he had first
captured, he now sang wilder songs, and passed
more flowing bowls, for this prize was a much
greater one than the first. If Bartholemy could
have communicated his great good fortune to the
other buccaneers in the West Indies, there would
have been a boom in piracy which would have
threatened great danger to the honesty and integ-
rity of the seafaring men of that region.

But nobody, not even a pirate, has any way of
finding out what is going to happen next, and if
Bartholemy had had an idea of the fluctuations
which were about to occur in the market in which
he had made his investments he would have been
in a great hurry to sell all his stock very much
below par. The fluctuations referred to occurred
on the ocean, near the island of Pinos, and came in
the shape of great storm waves, which blew the
Spanish vessel with all its rich cargo, and its triumphant pirate crew, high up upon the cruel rocks,
and wrecked it absolutely and utterly. Bartholemy
and his men barely managed to get into a little
boat, and row themselves away. All the wealth

and treasure which had come to them with the capture of the Spanish vessel, all the power which the
possession of that vessel gave them, and all the
wild joy which came to them with riches and power,
were lost to them in as short a space of time as it
had taken to gain them.

In the way of well-defined and conspicuous ups
and downs, few lives surpassed that of Bartholemy
Portuguez.   But after this he seems, in the language
of the old English song, " All in the downs."   He
had many adventures after the desperate affair in the
bay of Campeachy, but they must all have turned
out badly for him, and, consequently, very well, it is
probable, for divers and sundry Spanish vessels, and,
for the rest of his life, he bore the reputation of an
unfortunate pirate.   He was one of those men
whose success seemed to have depended entirely
upon his own exertions.   If there happened to be
the least chance of his doing anything, he generally
did it; Spanish cannon, well-armed Spanish crews,
manacles, imprisonment, the dangers of the ocean
to a man who could not swim, bloodhounds, alligators, wild beasts, awful forests impenetrable to common men, all these were bravely met and triumphed
over by Bartholemy.

But when he came to ordinary good fortune, such
as any pirate might expect, Bartholemy the Portuguese found that he had no chance at all.   But

he was not a common pirate, and was, therefore,
obliged to be content with his uncommon career.
He eventually settled in the island of Jamaica, but
nobody knows what became of him.  If it so happened that he found himself obliged to make his
living by some simple industry, such as the selling
of fruit upon a street corner, it is likely he never
disposed of a banana or an orange unless he jumped
at the throat of a passer-by and compelled him to
purchase.  As for sitting still and waiting for customers to come to him, such a man as Bartholemy
would not be likely to do anything so commonplace.

# Chapter IX

## A Pirate Author

IN the days which we are considering there were all sorts of pirates, some of whom gained much reputation in one way and some in another, but there was one of them who had a disposition different from that of any of his fellows. He was a regular pirate, but it is not likely that he ever did much fighting, for, as he took great pride in the brave deeds of the Brethren of the Coast, he would have been sure to tell us of his own if he had ever performed any. He was a mild-mannered man, and, although he was a pirate, he eventually laid aside the pistol, the musket, and the cutlass, and took up the pen, — a very uncommon weapon for a buccaneer.

This man was John Esquemeling, supposed by some to be a Dutchman, and by others a native of France. He sailed to the West Indies in the year 1666, in the service of the French West India Company. He went out as a peaceable merchant clerk, and had no more idea of becoming a pirate than he had of going into literature, although he finally did both.

At that time the French West India Company had a colonial establishment on the island of Tortuga, which was principally inhabited, as we have seen before, by buccaneers in all their various grades and stages, from beef-driers to pirates. The French authorities undertook to supply these erratic people with the goods and provisions which they needed, and built storehouses with everything necessary for carrying on the trade. There were plenty of purchasers, for the buccaneers were willing to buy everything which could be brought from Europe. They were fond of good wine, good groceries, good firearms, and ammunition, fine cutlasses, and very often good clothes, in which they could disport themselves when on shore. But they had peculiar customs and manners, and although they were willing to buy as much as the French traders had to sell, they could not be prevailed upon to pay their bills. A pirate is not the sort of a man who generally cares to pay his bills. When he gets goods in any way, he wants them charged to him, and if that charge includes the features of robbery and murder, he will probably make no objection. But as for paying good money for what is received, that is quite another thing.

That this was the state of feeling on the island

of Tortuga was discovered before very long by the French mercantile agents, who then applied to the mother country for assistance in collecting the debts due them, and a body of men, who might be called collectors, or deputy sheriffs, was sent out to the island ; but although these officers were armed with pistols and swords, as well as with authority, they could do nothing with the buccaneers, and after a time the work of endeavoring to collect debts from pirates was given up. And as there was no profit in carrying on business in this way, the mercantile agency was also given up, and its officers were ordered to sell out everything they had on hand, and come home. There was, therefore, a sale, for which cash payments were demanded, and there was a great bargain day on the island of Tortuga. Everything was disposed of, — the stock of merchandise on hand, the tables, the desks, the stationery, the bookkeepers, the clerks, and the errand boys. The living items of the stock on hand were considered to be property just as if they had been any kind of merchandise, and were sold as slaves.

Now poor John Esquemeling found himself in a sad condition. He was bought by one of the French officials who had been left on the island, and he described his new master as a veritable fiend. He was worked hard, half fed, treated cruelly in many ways, and to add to his misery, his

master tantalized him by offering to set him free
upon the payment of a sum of money equal to
about three hundred dollars.  He might as well
have been asked to pay three thousand or three
million dollars, for he had not a penny in the
world.

At last he was so fortunate as to fall sick, and
his master, as avaricious as he was cruel, fearing
that this creature he owned might die, and thus be
an entire loss to him, sold him to a surgeon, very
much as one would sell a sick horse to a veterinary
surgeon, on the principle that he might make something out of the animal by curing him.

His new master treated Esquemeling very well,
and after he had taken medicine and food enough
to set him upon his legs, and had worked for the
surgeon about a year, that kind master offered him
his liberty if he would promise, as soon as he could
earn the money, to pay him one hundred dollars,
which would be a profit to his owner, who had paid
but seventy dollars for him.  This offer, of course,
Esquemeling accepted with delight, and having
made the bargain, he stepped forth upon the warm
sands of the island of Tortuga a free and happy
man.  But he was as poor as a church mouse.
He had nothing in the world but the clothes on his
back, and he saw no way in which he could make
money enough to keep himself alive until he had

paid for himself. He tried various ways of support, but there was no opening for a young business man in that section of the country, and at last he came to the conclusion that there was only one way by which he could accomplish his object, and he therefore determined to enter into " the wicked order of pirates or robbers at sea."

It must have been a strange thing for a man accustomed to pens and ink, to yard-sticks and scales, to feel obliged to enroll himself into a company of bloody, big-bearded pirates, but a man must eat, and buccaneering was the only profession open to our ex-clerk. For some reason or other, certainly not on account of his bravery and daring, Esquemeling was very well received by the pirates of Tortuga. Perhaps they liked him because he was a mild-mannered man and so different from themselves. Nobody was afraid of him, every one felt superior to him, and we are all very apt to like people to whom we feel superior.

As for Esquemeling himself, he soon came to entertain the highest opinion of his pirate companions. He looked upon the buccaneers who had distinguished themselves as great heroes, and it must have been extremely gratifying to those savage fellows to tell Esquemeling all the wonderful things they had done. In the whole of the West Indies there was no one who was in the habit of giving such intelligent attention to the accounts of piratical depredations and savage sea-fights, as was Esquemeling, and if he had demanded a salary as a listener there is no doubt that it would have been paid to him.

It was not long before his intense admiration of the buccaneers and their performances began to produce in him the feeling that the history of these great exploits should not be lost to the world, and so he set about writing the lives and adventures of many of the buccaneers with whom he became acquainted.

He remained with the pirates for several years, and during that time worked very industriously getting material together for his history. When he returned to his own country in 1672, having done as much literary work as was possible among the uncivilized surroundings of Tortuga, he there completed a book, which he called, " The Buccaneers of America, or The True Account of the Most Remarkable Assaults Committed of Late Years Upon the Coasts of the West Indies by the Buccaneers, etc., by John Esquemeling, One of the Buccaneers, Who Was Present at Those Tragedies."

From this title it is probable that our literary pirate accompanied his comrades on their various voyages and assaults, in the capacity of reporter, and although he states he was present at many of

" those tragedies," he makes no reference to any deeds of valor or cruelty performed by himself, which shows him to have been a wonderfully conscientious historian. There are persons, however, who doubt his impartiality, because, as he liked the French, he always gave the pirates of that nationality the credit for most of the bravery displayed on their expeditions, and all of the magnanimity and courtesy, if there happened to be any, while the surliness, brutality, and extraordinary wickednesses were all ascribed to the English. But be this as it may, Esquemeling's history was a great success. It was written in Dutch and was afterwards translated into English, French, and Spanish. It contained a great deal of information regarding buccaneering in general, and most of the stories of pirates which we have already told, and many of the surprising narrations which are to come, have been taken from the book of this buccaneer historian.

# Chapter X

## The Story of Roc, the Brazilian

HAVING given the history of a very plain and quiet buccaneer, who was a reporter and writer, and who, if he were now living, would be eligible as a member of an Authors' Club, we will pass to the consideration of a regular out-and-out pirate, one from whose mast-head would have floated the black flag with its skull and cross-bones if that emblematic piece of bunting had been in use by the pirates of the period.

This famous buccaneer was called Roc, because he had to have a name, and his own was unknown, and "the Brazilian," because he was born in Brazil, though of Dutch parents. Unlike most of his fellow-practitioners he did not gradually become a pirate. From his early youth he never had an intention of being anything else. As soon as he grew to be a man he became a bloody buccaneer, and at the first opportunity he joined a pirate crew, and had made but a few voyages when it was perceived by his companions that he was destined to become a most remarkable sea-robber. He was offered the command of a ship with a well-armed crew of marine savages, and in a very short time after he had set out on his first independent cruise he fell in with a Spanish ship loaded with silver bullion; having captured this, he sailed with his prize to Jamaica, which was one of the great resorts of the English buccaneers. There his success delighted the community, his talents for the conduct of great piratical operations soon became apparent, and he was generally acknowledged as the Head Pirate of the West Indies.

He was now looked upon as a hero even by those colonists who had no sympathy with pirates, and as for Esquemeling, he simply worshipped the great Brazilian desperado. If he had been writing the life and times of Alexander the Great, Julius Cæsar, or Mr. Gladstone, he could not have been more enthusiastic in his praises. And as in The Arabian Nights the roc is described as the greatest of birds, so, in the eyes of the buccaneer biographer, this Roc was the greatest of pirates. But it was not only in the mind of the historian that Roc now became famous; the better he became known, the more general was the fear and respect felt for him, and we are told that the mothers of the islands used to put their children to sleep by threatening them with the terrible Roc if they did not close their eyes.

This story, however, I regard with a great deal of doubt; it has been told of Saladin and many other wicked and famous men, but I do not believe it is an easy thing to frighten a child into going to sleep. If I found it necessary to make a youngster take a nap, I should say nothing of the condition of affairs in Cuba or of the persecutions of the Armenians.

This renowned pirate from Brazil must have been a terrible fellow to look at. He was strong and brawny, his face was short and very wide, with high cheek-bones, and his expression probably resembled that of a pug dog. His eyebrows were enormously large and bushy, and from under them he glared at his mundane surroundings. He was not a man whose spirit could be quelled by looking him steadfastly in the eye. It was his custom in the daytime to walk about, carrying a drawn cutlass, resting easily upon his arm, edge up, very much as a fine gentleman carries his high silk hat, and any one who should impertinently stare or endeavor to quell his high spirits in any other way, would probably have felt the edge of that cutlass descending rapidly through his physical organism.

He was a man who insisted upon being obeyed, and if any one of his crew behaved improperly, or was even found idle, this strict and inexorable master would cut him down where he stood. But although he was so strict and exacting during the business sessions of his piratical year, by which I mean when he was cruising around after prizes, he was very much more disagreeable when he was taking a vacation. On his return to Jamaica after one of his expeditions it was his habit to give himself some relaxation after the hardships and dangers through which he had passed, and on such occasions it was a great comfort to Roc to get himself thoroughly drunk. With his cutlass waving high in the air, he would rush out into the street and take a whack at every one whom he met. As far as was possible the citizens allowed him to have the street to himself, and it was not at all likely that his visits to Jamaica were looked forward to with any eager anticipations.

Roc, it may be said, was not only a bloody pirate, but a blooded one; he was thoroughbred. From the time he had been able to assert his individuality he had been a pirate, and there was no reason to suppose that he would ever reform himself into anything else. There were no extenuating circumstances in his case; in his nature there was no alloy, nor moderation, nor forbearance. The appreciative Esquemeling, who might be called the Boswell of the buccaneers, could never have met his hero Roc, when that bushy-bearded pirate was running "amuck" in the streets, but if he had, it is not probable that his book would have been written. He assures us that when Roc was not drunk he was esteemed, but at the same time feared; but there are various ways of gaining esteem, and Roc's method certainly succeeded very well in the case of his literary associate.

As we have seen, the hatred of the Spaniards by the buccaneers began very early in the settlement of the West Indies, and in fact, it is very likely that if there had been no Spaniards there would never have been any buccaneers; but in all the instances of ferocious enmity toward the Spaniards there has been nothing to equal the feelings of Roc, the Brazilian, upon that subject. His dislike to everything Spanish arose, he declared, from cruelties which had been practised upon his parents by people of that nation, and his main principle of action throughout all his piratical career seems to have been that there was nothing too bad for a Spaniard. The object of his life was to wage bitter war against Spanish ships and Spanish settlements. He seldom gave any quarter to his prisoners, and would often subject them to horrible tortures in order to make them tell where he could find the things he wanted. There is nothing horrible that has ever been written or told about the buccaneer life, which could not have been told about Roc, the Brazilian. He was a typical pirate.

Roc was very successful in his enterprises, and took a great deal of valuable merchandise to Jamaica, but although he and his crew were always rich men

"In a small boat filled with some of his trusty men, he rowed
quietly into the port." — p. 77.

when they went on shore, they did not remain in that condition very long. The buccaneers of that day were all very extravagant, and, moreover, they were great gamblers, and it was not uncommon for them to lose everything they possessed before they had been on shore a week. Then there was nothing for them to do but to go on board their vessels and put out to sea in search of some fresh prize. So far Roc's career had been very much like that of many other Companions of the Coast, differing from them only in respect to intensity and force, but he was a clever man with ideas, and was able to adapt himself to circumstances.

He was cruising about Campeachy without seeing any craft that was worth capturing, when he thought that it would be very well for him to go out on a sort of marine scouting expedition and find out whether or not there were any Spanish vessels in the bay which were well laden and which were likely soon to come out. So, with a small boat filled with some of his trusty men, he rowed quietly into the port to see what he could discover. If he had had Esquemeling with him, and had sent that mild-mannered observer into the harbor to investigate into the state of affairs, and come back with a report, it would have been a great deal better for the pirate captain, but he chose to go himself, and he came to grief. No sooner did the people on the

ships lying in the harbor behold a boat approaching
with a big-browed, broad-jawed mariner sitting in
the stern, and with a good many more broad-backed,
hairy mariners than were necessary, pulling at the
oars, than they gave the alarm.   The well-known
pirate was recognized, and it was not long before he
was captured.   Roc must have had a great deal of
confidence in his own powers, or perhaps he relied
somewhat upon the fear which his very presence
evoked.   But he made a mistake this time; he had
run into the lion's jaw, and the lion had closed his
teeth upon him.

When the pirate captain and his companions
were brought before the Governor, he made no
pretence of putting them to trial.   Buccaneers were
outlawed by the Spanish, and were considered as
wild beasts to be killed without mercy wherever
caught.   Consequently Roc and his men were
thrown into a dungeon and condemned to be executed.   If, however, the Spanish Governor had
known what was good for himself, he would have
had them killed that night.

During the time that preparations were going on
for making examples of these impertinent pirates,
who had dared to enter the port of Campeachy,
Roc was racking his brains to find some method
of getting out of the terrible scrape into which he
had fallen.   This was a branch of the business in

which a capable pirate was obliged to be proficient;
if he could not get himself out of scrapes, he could
not expect to be successful. In this case there was
no chance of cutting down sentinels, or jumping
overboard with a couple of wine-jars for a life-preserver, or of doing any of those ordinary things
which pirates were in the habit of doing when escaping from their captors. Roc and his men were in
a dungeon on land, inside of a fortress, and if they
escaped from this, they would find themselves unarmed in the midst of a body of Spanish soldiers.
Their stout arms and their stout hearts were of no
use to them now, and they were obliged to depend
upon their wits if they had any. Roc had plenty of
wit, and he used it well. There was a slave, probably not a negro nor a native, but most likely some
European who had been made prisoner, who came
in to bring him food and drink, and by the means
of this man the pirate hoped to play a trick upon
the Governor. He promised the slave that if he
would help him, — and he told him it would be very
easy to do so, — he would give him money enough
to buy his freedom and to return to his friends, and
this, of course, was a great inducement to the poor
fellow, who may have been an Englishman or a
Frenchman in good circumstances at home. The
slave agreed to the proposals, and the first thing he
did was to bring some writing-materials to Roc, who

thereupon began the composition of a letter upon
which he based all his hopes of life and freedom.

When he was coming into the bay, Roc had no-
ticed a large French vessel that was lying at some distance from the town, and he wrote his letter as if it
had come from the captain of this ship. In the character of this French captain he addressed his letter to
the Governor of the town, and in it he stated that he
had understood that certain Companions of the Coast,
for whom he had great sympathy, — for the French
and the buccaneers were always good friends, —
had been captured by the Governor, who, he heard,
had threatened to execute them. Then the French
captain, by the hand of Roc, went on to say that if
any harm should come to these brave men, who
had been taken and imprisoned when they were
doing no harm to anybody, he would swear, in his
most solemn manner, that never, for the rest of his
life, would he give quarter to any Spaniard who
might fall into his hands, and he, moreover, threatened that any kind of vengeance which should
become possible for the buccaneers and French
united, to inflict upon the Spanish ships, or upon
the town of Campeachy, should be taken as soon
as possible after he should hear of any injury that
might be inflicted upon the unfortunate men who
were then lying imprisoned in the fortress.

When the slave came back to Roc, the letter was

" When the slave came back to Roc, the letter was given to him
with very particular directions."— p. 80.

given to him with very particular directions as to what he was to do with it. He was to disguise himself as much as possible, so that he should not be recognized by the people of the place, and then in the night he was to make his way out of the town, and early in the morning he was to return as if he had been walking along the shore of the harbor, when he was to state that he had been put on shore from the French vessel in the offing, with a letter which he was to present to the Governor.

The slave performed his part of the business very well. The next day, wet and bedraggled, from making his way through the weeds and mud of the coast, he presented himself at the fortress with his letter, and when he was allowed to take it to the Governor, no one suspected that he was a person employed about the place. Having fulfilled his mission, he departed, and when seen again he was the same servant whose business it was to carry food to the prisoners.

The Governor read the letter with a disquieted mind; he knew that the French ship which was lying outside the harbor was a powerful vessel and he did not like French ships, anyway. The town had once been taken and very badly treated by a little fleet of French and English buccaneers, and he was very anxious that nothing of the kind should happen again. There was no great Spanish force in

the harbor at that time, and he did not know how
many buccaneering vessels might be able to gather
together in the bay if it should become known that
the great pirate Roc had been put to death in Campeachy. It was an unusual thing for a prisoner to
have such powerful friends so near by, and the Governor took Roc's case into most earnest consideration. A few hours' reflection was sufficient to
convince him that it would be very unsafe to tamper
with such a dangerous prize as the pirate Roc, and
he determined to get rid of him as soon as possible.
He felt himself in the position of a man who has
stolen a baby-bear, and who hears the roar of an
approaching parent through the woods ; to throw
away the cub and walk off as though he had no idea
there were any bears in that forest would be the
inclination of a man so situated, and to get rid of
the great pirate without provoking the vengeance
of his friends was the natural inclination of the
Governor.

Now Roc and his men were treated well, and
having been brought before the Governor, were told
that in consequence of their having committed no
overt act of disorder they would be set at liberty
and shipped to England, upon the single condition
that they would abandon piracy and agree to become quiet citizens in whatever respectable vocation
they might select.

To these terms Roc and his men agreed without argument. They declared that they would retire from the buccaneering business, and that nothing would suit them better than to return to the ways of civilization and virtue. There was a ship about to depart for Spain, and on this the Governor gave Roc and his men free passage to the other side of the ocean. There is no doubt that our buccaneers would have much preferred to have been put on board the French vessel; but as the Spanish Governor had started his prisoners on the road to reform, he did not wish to throw them into the way of temptation by allowing them to associate with such wicked companions as Frenchmen, and Roc made no suggestion of the kind, knowing very well how greatly astonished the French captain would be if the Governor were to communicate with him on the subject.

On the voyage to Spain Roc was on his good behavior, and he was a man who knew how to behave very well when it was absolutely necessary: no doubt there must have been many dull days on board ship when he would have been delighted to gamble, to get drunk, and to run "amuck" up and down the deck. But he carefully abstained from all these recreations, and showed himself to be such an able-bodied and willing sailor that the captain allowed him to serve as one of the crew. Roc knew

how to do a great many things ; not only could he
murder and rob, but he knew how to turn an honest
penny when there was no other way of filling his
purse.   He had learned among the Indians how to
shoot fish with bow and arrows, and on this voyage
across the Atlantic he occupied all his spare time in
sitting in the rigging and shooting the fish which
disported themselves about the vessel.   These fish
he sold to the officers, and we are told that in this
way he earned no less than five hundred crowns,
perhaps that many dollars.   If this account is true,
fish must have been very costly in those days, but
it showed plainly that if Roc had desired to get
into an honest business, he would have found fish-
shooting a profitable occupation.   In every way Roc
behaved so well that for his sake all his men were
treated kindly and allowed many privileges.

But when this party of reformed pirates reached
Spain and were allowed to go where they pleased,
they thought no more of the oaths they had taken
to abandon piracy than they thought of the oaths
which they had been in the habit of throwing right
and left when they had been strolling about on the
island of Jamaica.   They had no ship, and not
enough money to buy one, but as soon as they could
manage it they sailed back to the West Indies, and
eventually found themselves in Jamaica, as bold and
as bloody buccaneers as ever they had been.

Not only did Roc cast from him every thought of reformation and a respectable life, but he determined to begin the business of piracy on a grander scale than ever before. He made a compact with an old French buccaneer, named Tributor, and with a large company of buccaneers he actually set out to take a town. Having lost everything he possessed, and having passed such a long time without any employment more profitable than that of shooting fish with a bow and arrows, our doughty pirate now desired to make a grand strike, and if he could take a town and pillage it of everything valuable it contained, he would make a very good fortune in a very short time, and might retire, if he chose, from the active practice of his profession.

The town which Roc and Tributor determined to attack was Merida, in Yucatan, and although this was a bold and rash undertaking, the two pirates were bold and rash enough for anything. Roc had been a prisoner in Merida, and on account of his knowledge of the town he believed that he and his followers could land upon the coast, and then quietly advance upon the town without their approach being discovered. If they could do this, it would be an easy matter to rush upon the unsuspecting garrison, and, having annihilated these, make themselves masters of the town.

But their plans did not work very well; they

were discovered by some Indians, after they had landed, who hurried to Merida and gave notice of the approach of the buccaneers. Consequently, when Roc and his companions reached the town they found the garrison prepared for them, cannons loaded, and all the approaches guarded. Still the pirates did not hesitate; they advanced fiercely to the attack just as they were accustomed to do when they were boarding a Spanish vessel, but they soon found that fighting on land was very different from fighting at sea. In a marine combat it is seldom that a party of boarders is attacked in the rear by the enemy, although on land such methods of warfare may always be expected; but Roc and Tributor did not expect anything of the kind, and they were, therefore, greatly dismayed when a party of horsemen from the town, who had made a wide détour through the woods, suddenly charged upon their rear. Between the guns of the garrison and the sabres of the horsemen the buccaneers had a very hard time, and it was not long before they were completely defeated. Tributor and a great many of the pirates were killed or taken, and Roc, the Brazilian, had a terrible fall.

This most memorable fall occurred in the estimation of John Esquemeling, who knew all about the attack on Merida, and who wrote the account of it. But he had never expected to be called upon to record that his great hero, Roc, the Brazilian, saved his life, after the utter defeat of himself and his companions, by ignominiously running away. The loyal chronicler had as firm a belief in the absolute inability of his hero to fly from danger as was shown by the Scottish Douglas, when he stood, his back against a mass of stone, and invited his enemies to " Come one, come all." The bushy-browed pirate of the drawn cutlass had so often expressed his contempt for a soldier who would even surrender, to say nothing of running away, that Esquemeling could scarcely believe that Roc had retreated from his enemies, deserted his friends, and turned his back upon the principles which he had always so truculently proclaimed.

But this downfall of a hero simply shows that Esquemeling, although he was a member of the piratical body, and was proud to consider himself a buccaneer, did not understand the true nature of a pirate. Under the brutality, the cruelty, the dishonesty, and the recklessness of the sea-robbers of those days, there was nearly always meanness and cowardice. Roc, as we have said in the beginning of this sketch, was a typical pirate; under certain circumstances he showed himself to have all those brave and savage qualities which Esquemeling esteemed and revered, and under other circumstances he showed those other qualities which Esquemeling despised, but which are necessary to make up the true character of a pirate.

The historian John seems to have been very much cut up by the manner in which his favorite hero had rounded off his piratical career, and after that he entirely dropped Roc from his chronicles.

This out-and-out pirate was afterwards living in Jamaica, and probably engaged in new enterprises, but Esquemeling would have nothing more to do with him nor with the history of his deeds.

# Chapter XI

## A Buccaneer Boom

THE condition of affairs in the West Indies was becoming very serious in the eyes of the Spanish rulers. They had discovered a new country, they had taken possession of it, and they had found great wealth of various kinds, of which they were very much in need. This wealth was being carried to Spain as fast as it could be taken from the unfortunate natives and gathered together for transportation, and everything would have gone on very well indeed had it not been for the most culpable and unwarranted interference of that lawless party of men, who might almost be said to amount to a nationality, who were continually on the alert to take from Spain everything she could take from America. The English, French, and Dutch governments were generally at peace with Spain, but they sat by quietly and saw their sailor subjects band themselves together and make war upon Spanish commerce, — a very one-sided commerce, it is true.

It was of no use for Spain to complain of the
buccaneers to her sister maritime nations. It is not
certain that they could have done anything to interfere with the operations of the sea-robbers who
originally sailed from their coasts, but it is certain
they did not try to do anything. Whatever was
to be done, Spain must do herself. The pirates
were as slippery as they were savage, and although
the Spaniards made a regular naval war upon them,
they seemed to increase rather than to diminish.
Every time that a Spanish merchantman was taken,
and its gold and silver and valuable goods carried
off to Tortuga or Jamaica, and divided among a lot
of savage and rollicking fellows, the greater became
the enthusiasm among the Brethren of the Coast,
and the wider spread the buccaneering boom. More
ships laden almost entirely with stalwart men, well
provided with arms, and very badly furnished with
principles, came from England and France, and the
Spanish ships of war in the West Indies found that
they were confronted by what was, in many respects,
a regular naval force.

The buccaneers were afraid of nothing; they paid
no attention to the rules of war,—a little ship would
attack a big one without the slightest hesitation,
and more than that, would generally take it,—and
in every way Spain was beginning to feel as if she
were acting the part of provider to the pirate seamen of every nation.

Finding that she could do nothing to diminish the number of the buccaneering vessels, Spain determined that she would not have so many richly laden ships of her own upon these dangerous seas; consequently, a change was made in regard to the shipping of merchandise and the valuable metals from America to her home ports. The cargoes were concentrated, and what had previously been placed upon three ships was crowded into the holds and between the decks of one great vessel, which was so well armed and defended as to make it almost impossible for any pirate ship to capture it. In some respects this plan worked very well, although when the buccaneers did happen to pounce upon one of these richly laden vessels, in such numbers and with such swift ferocity, that they were able to capture it, they rejoiced over a prize far more valuable than anything the pirate soul had ever dreamed of before. But it was not often that one of these great ships was taken, and for a time the results of Spanish robbery and cruelty were safely carried to Spain.

But it was very hard to get the better of the buccaneers; their lives and their fortunes depended upon this boom, and if in one way they could not get the gold out of the Spaniards, which the latter got out of the natives, they would try another. When the miners in the gold fields find they can no longer wash out with their pans a paying quan-

tity of the precious metal, they go to work on the
rocks and break them into pieces and crush them
into dust; so, when the buccaneers found it did not
pay to devote themselves to capturing Spanish gold
on its transit across the ocean, many of them changed
their methods of operation and boldly planned to
seize the treasures of their enemy before it was put
upon the ships.

Consequently, the buccaneers formed themselves
into larger bodies commanded by noted leaders, and
made attacks upon the Spanish settlements and
towns. Many of these were found nearly defenceless, and even those which boasted fortifications
often fell before the reckless charges of the buccaneers. The pillage, the burning, and the cruelty on
shore exceeded that which had hitherto been known
on the sea. There is generally a great deal more in
a town than there is in a ship, and the buccaneers
proved themselves to be among the most outrageous, exacting, and cruel conquerors ever known in
the world. They were governed by no laws of warfare; whatever they chose to do they did. They
respected nobody, not even themselves, and acted
like wild beasts, without the disposition which is
generally shown by a wild beast, to lie down and go
to sleep when he has had enough.

There were times when it seemed as though it
would be safer for a man who had a regard for his

life and comfort, to sail upon a pirate ship instead of a Spanish galleon, or to take up his residence in one of the uncivilized communities of Tortuga or Jamaica, instead of settling in a well-ordered Spanish-American town with its mayor, its officials, and its garrison.

It was a very strange nation of marine bandits which had thus sprung into existence on these far-away waters; it was a nation of grown-up men, who existed only for the purpose of carrying off that which other people were taking away; it was a nation of second-hand robbers, who carried their operations to such an extent that they threatened to do away entirely with that series of primary robberies to which Spain had devoted herself. I do not know that there were any companies formed in those days for the prosecution of buccaneering, but I am quite sure that if there had been, their shares would have gone up to a very high figure.

# Chapter XII

## The Story of L'Olonnois the Cruel

IN the preceding chapter we have seen that the buccaneers had at last become so numerous and so formidable that it was dangerous for a Spanish ship laden with treasure from the new world to attempt to get out of the Caribbean Sea into the Atlantic, and that thus failing to find enough richly laden vessels to satisfy their ardent cravings for plunder, the buccaneers were forced to make some change in their methods of criminal warfare; and from capturing Spanish galleons, they formed themselves into well-organized bodies and attacked towns.

Among the buccaneer leaders who distinguished themselves as land pirates was a thoroughbred scoundrel by the name of Francis L'Olonnois, who was born in France. In those days it was the custom to enforce servitude upon people who were not able to take care of themselves. Unfortunate debtors and paupers of all classes were sold to people who had need of their services. The only difference sometimes between master and servant depended entirely upon the fact that one had money, and the other had none. Boys and girls were sold for a term of years, somewhat as if they had been apprentices, and it so happened that the boy L'Olonnois was sold to a master who took him to the West Indies. There he led the life of a slave until he was of age, and then, being no longer subject to ownership, he became one of the freest and most independent persons who ever walked this earth.

He began his career on the island of Hispaniola, where he took up the business of hunting and butchering cattle; but he very soon gave up this life for that of a pirate, and enlisted as a common sailor on one of their ships. Here he gave signs of such great ability as a brave and unscrupulous scoundrel that one of the leading pirates on the island of Tortuga gave him a ship and a crew, and set him up in business on his own account. The piratical career of L'Olonnois was very much like that of other buccaneers of the day, except that he was so abominably cruel to the Spanish prisoners whom he captured that he gained a reputation for vile humanity, surpassing that of any other rascal on the western continent. When he captured a prisoner, it seemed to delight his soul as much to torture and mutilate him before killing him as to take away whatever valuables he possessed. His

reputation for ingenious wickedness spread all over
the West Indies, so that the crews of Spanish ships,
attacked by this demon, would rather die on their
decks or sink to the bottom in their ships than be
captured by L'Olonnois.

All the barbarities, the brutalities, and the fiend-
ish ferocity which have ever been attributed to the
pirates of the world were united in the character of
this inhuman wretch, who does not appear to be so
good an example of the true pirate as Roc, the
Brazilian. He was not so brave, he was not so
able, and he was so utterly base that it would be
impossible for any one to look upon him as a hero.
After having attained in a very short time the reputation of being the most bloody and wicked pirate
of his day, L'Olonnois was unfortunate enough to
be wrecked upon the coast, not far from the town
of Campeachy. He and his crew got safely to
shore, but it was not long before their presence
was discovered by the people of the town, and the
Spanish soldiers thereupon sallied out and attacked
them. There was a fierce fight, but the Spaniards
were the stronger, and the buccaneers were utterly
defeated. Many of them were killed, and most of
the rest wounded or taken prisoners.

Among the wounded was L'Olonnois, and as he
knew that if he should be discovered he would
meet with no mercy, he got behind some bushes,

scooped up several handfuls of sand, mixed it with his blood, and with it rubbed his face so that it presented the pallor of a corpse. Then he lay down among the bodies of his dead companions, and when the Spaniards afterwards walked over the battlefield, he was looked upon as one of the common pirates whom they had killed.

When the soldiers had retired into the town with their prisoners, the make-believe corpse stealthily arose and made his way into the woods, where he stayed until his wounds were well enough for him to walk about. He divested himself of his great boots, his pistol belt, and the rest of his piratical costume, and, adding to his scanty raiment a cloak and hat which he had stolen from a poor cottage, he boldly approached the town and entered it. He looked like a very ordinary person, and no notice was taken of him by the authorities. Here he found shelter and something to eat, and he soon began to make himself very much at home in the streets of Campeachy.

It was a very gay time in the town, and, as everybody seemed to be happy, L'Olonnois was very glad to join in the general rejoicing, and these hilarities gave him particular pleasure as he found out that he was the cause of them. The buccaneers who had been captured, and who were imprisoned in the fortress, had been interrogated over and

over again by the Spanish officials in regard to
L'Olonnois, their commander, and, as they had
invariably answered that he had been killed, the
Spanish were forced to believe the glad tidings, and
they celebrated the death of the monster as the
greatest piece of public good fortune which could
come to their community. They built bonfires,
they sang songs about the death of the black-hearted
buccaneer, and services of thanksgiving were held in
their churches.

All this was a great delight to L'Olonnois, who
joined hands with the young men and women, as
they danced around the bonfires; he assisted in a
fine bass voice in the choruses which told of his
death and his dreadful doom, and he went to church
and listened to the priests and the people as they gave
thanks for their deliverance from his enormities.

But L'Olonnois did not waste all his time
chuckling over the baseless rejoicings of the people
of the town. He made himself acquainted with
some of the white slaves, men who had been brought
from England, and finding some of them very
much discontented with their lot, he ventured to
tell them that he was one of the pirates who had
escaped, and offered them riches and liberty if they
would join him in a scheme he had concocted. It
would have been easy enough for him to get away
from the town by himself, but this would have been

of no use to him unless he obtained some sort of a
vessel, and some men to help him navigate it.    So
he proposed to the slaves that they should steal a
small boat belonging to the master of one of them,
and in this, under cover of the night, the little
party safely left Campeachy and set sail for Tortuga,
which, as we have told, was then the headquarters
of the buccaneers, and " the common place of refuge
of all sorts of wickedness, and the seminary, as it
were, of all manner of pirates."

# Chapter XIII

## A Resurrected Pirate

WHEN L'Olonnois arrived at Tortuga he caused great astonishment among his old associates; that he had come back a comparative pauper surprised no one, for this was a common thing to happen to a pirate, but the wonder was that he got back at all.

He had no money, but, by the exercise of his crafty abilities, he managed to get possession of a ship, which he manned with a crew of about a score of impecunious dare-devils who were very anxious to do something to mend their fortunes.

Having now become very fond of land-fighting, he did not go out in search of ships, but directed his vessel to a little village called de los Cayos, on the coast of Cuba, for here, he thought, was a chance for a good and easy stroke of business. This village was the abode of industrious people, who were traders in tobacco, hides, and sugar, and who were obliged to carry on their traffic in a rather peculiar manner. The sea near their town was shallow, so that large ships could not approach very near, and thus the villagers were kept busy carrying goods and supplies in small boats, backwards and forwards from the town to the vessels at anchor. Here was a nice little prize that could not get away from him, and L'Olonnois had plenty of time to make his preparations to seize it. As he could not sail a ship directly up to the town, he cruised about the coast at some distance from de los Cayos, endeavoring to procure two small boats in which to approach the town, but although his preparations were made as quietly as possible, the presence of his vessel was discovered by some fishermen. They knew that it was a pirate ship, and some of them who had seen L'Olonnois recognized that dreaded pirate upon the deck. Word of the impending danger was taken to the town, and the people there immediately sent a message by land to Havana, informing the Governor of the island that the cruel pirate L'Olonnois was in a ship a short distance from their village, which he undoubtedly intended to attack.

When the Governor heard this astonishing tale, it was almost impossible for him to believe it. The good news of the death of L'Olonnois had come from Campeachy to Havana, and the people of the latter town also rejoiced greatly. To be now told that this scourge of the West Indies was alive, and was about to fall upon a peaceful little village on the

island over which he ruled, filled the Governor with
rage as well as amazement, and he ordered a well-
armed ship, with a large crew of fighting men, to
sail immediately for de los Cayos, giving the captain
express orders that he was not to come back until
he had obliterated from the face of the earth the
whole of the wretched gang with the exception of
the leader. This extraordinary villain was to be
brought to Havana to be treated as the Governor
should see fit. In order that his commands should
be executed promptly and effectually, the Governor
sent a big negro slave in the ship, who was charged
with the duty of hanging every one of the pirates
except L'Olonnois.

By the time the war-vessel had arrived at de los
Cayos, L'Olonnois had made his preparation to
attack the place. He had procured two large canoes,
and in these he had intended to row up to the town
and land with his men. But now there was a change
in the state of affairs, and he was obliged to alter
his plans. The ordinary person in command of two
small boats, who should suddenly discover that a
village which he supposed almost defenceless, was
protected by a large man-of-war, with cannon and a
well-armed crew, would have altered his plans so
completely that he would have left that part of the
coast of Cuba with all possible expedition. But
the pirates of that day seemed to pay very little

attention to the element of odds; if they met an
enemy who was weak, they would fall upon him,
and if they met with one who was a good deal
stronger than themselves, they would fall upon him
all the same. When the time came to fight they
fought.

Of course L'Olonnois could not now row leisurely
up to the town and begin to pillage it as he had
intended, but no intention of giving up his project
entered his mind. As the Spanish vessel was in
his way, he would attack her and get her out of his
way if the thing could be done.

In this new state of affairs he was obliged to use
stratagem, and he also needed a larger force than he
had with him, and he therefore captured some men
who were fishing along the coast and put them into
his canoes to help work the oars. Then by night
he proceeded slowly in the direction of the Spanish
vessel. The man-of-war was anchored not very far
from the town, and when about two o'clock in the
morning the watch on deck saw some canoes approaching they supposed them to be boats from
shore, for, as has been said, such vessels were continually plying about those shallow waters. The
canoes were hailed, and after having given an account
of themselves they were asked if they knew anything
about the pirate ship upon the coast. L'Olonnois
understood very well that it would not do for him

or his men to make answer to these inquiries, for
their speech would have shown they did not belong
to those parts.    Therefore he made one of his
prisoner fishermen answer that they had not seen a
pirate vessel, and if there had been one there, it
must have sailed away when its captain heard the
Spanish ship was coming.    Then the canoes were
allowed to go their way, but their way was a very
different one from any which could have been expected by the captain of the ship.

They rowed off into the darkness instead of going
toward the town, and waited until nearly daybreak,
then they boldly made for the man-of-war, one
canoe attacking her on one side and the other on the
other.    Before the Spanish could comprehend what
had happened there were more than twenty pirates
upon their decks, the dreaded L'Olonnois at their
head.

In such a case as this cannon were of no use, and
when the crew tried to rush upon deck, they found
that cutlasses and pistols did not avail very much
better.    The pirates had the advantage; they had
overpowered the watch, and were defending the deck
against all comers from below.    It requires a very
brave sailor to stick his head out of a hatchway
when he sees three or four cutlasses ready to split it
open.    But there was some stout fighting on board;
the officers came out of their cabins, and some of the

men were able to force their way out into the
struggle. The pirates knew, however, that they
were but few and that were their enemies allowed to
get on deck they would prove entirely too strong,
and they fought, each scoundrel of them, like three
men, and the savage fight ended by every Spanish
sailor or officer who was not killed or wounded
being forced to stay below decks, where the hatches
were securely fastened down upon them.

L'Olonnois now stood a proud victor on the deck
of his prize, and, being a man of principle, he determined to live up to the distinguished reputation
which he had acquired in that part of the world.
Baring his muscular and hairy right arm, he clutched
the handle of his sharp and heavy cutlass and ordered the prisoners to be brought up from below,
one at a time, and conducted to the place where he
stood. He wished to give Spain a lesson which
would make her understand that he was not to be
interfered with in the execution of his enterprises,
and he determined to allow himself the pleasure of
personally teaching this lesson.

As soon as a prisoner was brought to L'Olonnois
he struck off his head, and this performance he
continued, beginning with number one, and going
on until he had counted ninety. The last one
brought to him was the negro slave. This man,
who was not a soldier, was desperately frightened

and begged piteously for his life. L'Olonnois, finding that the man was willing to tell everything he
knew, questioned him about the sending of this
vessel from Havana, and when the poor fellow had
finished by telling that he had come there, not of
his own accord, but simply for the purpose of obey-
ing his master, to hang all the pirates except their
leader, that great buccaneer laughed, and, finding
he could get nothing more from the negro, cut off
his head likewise, and his body was tumbled into
the sea after those of his companions.

Now there was not a Spaniard left on board the
great ship except one man, who had been preserved
from the fate of the others because L'Olonnois had
some correspondence to attend to, and he needed a
messenger to carry a letter. The pirate captain
went into the cabin, where he found writing-materials ready to his hand, and there he composed a
letter to the Governor of Havana, a part of which
read as follows: "I shall never henceforward give
quarter unto any Spaniard whatsoever. And I have
great hopes that I shall execute on your own person
the very same punishment I have done to them you
sent against me. Thus I have retaliated the kindness you designed unto me and my companions."

When this message was received by the dignified
official who filled the post of Governor of Cuba, he
stormed and fairly foamed at the mouth. To be

utterly foiled and discomfited by this resurrected pirate, and to be afterwards addressed in terms of such unheard-of insolence and abuse, was more than he could bear, and, in the presence of many of his officials and attendants, he swore a terrible oath that after that hour he would never again give quarter to any buccaneer, no matter when or where he was captured, or what he might be doing at the time. Every man of the wretched band should die as soon as he could lay hands upon him.

But when the inhabitants of Havana and the surrounding villages heard of this terrible resolution of their Governor they were very much disturbed. They lived in constant danger of attack, especially those who were engaged in fishing or maritime pursuits, and they feared that when it became known that no buccaneer was to receive quarter, the Spanish colonists would be treated in the same way, no matter where they might be found and taken. Consequently, it was represented to the Governor that his plan of vengeance would work most disastrously for the Spanish settlers, for the buccaneers could do far more damage to them than he could possibly do to these dreadful Brethren of the Coast, and that, unless he wished to bring upon them troubles greater than those of famine or pestilence, they begged that he would retract his oath.

When the high dignitary had cooled down a

little, he saw that there was a good deal of sense in what the representative of the people had said to him, and he consequently felt obliged, in consideration of the public safety, to take back what he had said, and to give up the purpose, which would have rendered unsafe the lives of so many peaceable people.

L'Olonnois was now the possessor of a fine vessel which had not been in the least injured during the battle in which it had been won. But his little crew, some of whom had been killed and wounded, was insufficient to work such a ship upon an important cruise on the high seas, and he also discovered, much to his surprise, that there were very few provisions on board, for when the vessel was sent from Havana it was supposed she would make but a very short cruise. This savage swinger of the cutlass thereupon concluded that he would not try to do any great thing for the present, but, having obtained some booty and men from the woe-begone town of de los Cayos, he sailed away, touching at several other small ports for the purpose of pillage, and finally anchoring at Tortuga.

# Chapter XIV

## Villany on a Grand Scale

WHEN L'Olonnois landed on the disreputable shores of Tortuga, he was received by all circles of the vicious society of the island with loud acclamation. He had not only taken a fine Spanish ship, he had not only bearded the Governor of Havana in his fortified den, but he had struck off ninety heads with his own hand. Even people who did not care for him before reverenced him now. In all the annals of piracy no hero had ever done such a deed as this, and the best records of human butchering had been broken.

Now grand and ambitious ideas began to swell the head of this champion slaughterer, and he conceived the plan of getting up a grand expedition to go forth and capture the important town of Maracaibo, in New Venezuela. This was an enterprise far above the ordinary aims of a buccaneer, and it would require more than ordinary force to accomplish it. He therefore set himself to work to enlist a large number of men and to equip a fleet of vessels, of which he was to be chief commander or admiral. There were a great many unemployed pirates in Tortuga at that time, and many a brawny rascal volunteered to sail under the flag of the daring butcher of the seas.

But in order to equip a fleet, money was necessary as well as men, and therefore L'Olonnois thought himself very lucky when he succeeded in interesting the principal piratical capitalist of Tortuga in his undertaking. This was an old and seasoned buccaneer by the name of Michael de Basco, who had made money enough by his piratical exploits to retire from business and live on his income. He held the position of Mayor of the island and was an important man among his fellow-miscreants. When de Basco heard of the great expedition which L'Olonnois was about to undertake, his whole soul was fired and he could not rest tamely in his comfortable quarters when such great things were to be done, and he offered to assist L'Olonnois with funds and join in the expedition if he were made commander of the land forces. This offer was accepted gladly, for de Basco had a great reputation as a fighter in Europe as well as in America.

When everything had been made ready, L'Olonnois set sail for Maracaibo with a fleet of eight ships. On the way they captured two Spanish vessels, both of which were rich prizes, and at last they arrived before the town which they intended to capture.

Maracaibo was a prosperous place of three or four thousand inhabitants ; they were rich people living in fine houses, and many of them had plantations which extended out into the country. In every way the town possessed great attractions to piratical marauders, but there were difficulties in the way; being such an important place, of course it had important defences. On an island in the harbor there was a strong fort, or castle, and on another island a little further from the town there was a tall tower, on the top of which a sentinel was posted night and day to give notice of any approaching enemy. Between these two islands was the only channel by which the town could be approached from the sea. But in preparing these defences the authorities had thought only of defending themselves against ordinary naval forces and had not anticipated the extraordinary naval methods of the buccaneers who used to be merely sea-robbers, who fell upon ships after they had left their ports, but who now set out to capture not only ships at sea but towns on land.

L'Olonnois had too much sense to run his ships close under the guns of the fortress, against which he could expect to do nothing, for the buccaneers relied but little upon their cannon, and so they paid no more attention to the ordinary harbor than if it had not been there, but sailed into a fresh-water lake at some distance from the town, and out of sight of the tower. There L'Olonnois landed his men, and, advancing upon the fort from the rear, easily crossed over to the little island and marched upon the fort. It was very early in the morning. The garrison was utterly amazed by this attack from land, and although they fought bravely for three hours, they were obliged to give up the defence of the walls, and as many of them as could do so got out of the fort and escaped to the mainland and the town.

L'Olonnois now took possession of the fort, and then, with the greater part of his men, he returned to his ships, brought them around to the entrance of the bay, and then boldly sailed with his whole fleet under the very noses of the cannon and anchored in the harbor in front of the town.

When the citizens of Maracaibo heard from the escaping garrison that the fort had been taken, they were filled with horror and dismay, for they had no further means of defence. They knew that the pirates had come there for no other object than to rob, pillage, and cruelly treat them, and consequently as many as possible hurried away into the woods and the surrounding country with as many of their valuables as they could carry. They re-

sembled the citizens of a town attacked by the
cholera or the plague, and in fact, they would have
preferred a most terrible pestilence to this terrible
scourge of piracy from which they were about to
suffer.

As soon as L'Olonnois and his wild pirates had
landed in the city they devoted themselves entirely to
eating and drinking and making themselves merry.
They had been on short commons during the latter
part of their voyage, and they had a royal time with
the abundance of food and wine which they found in
the houses of the town.    The next day, however,
they set about attending to the business which had
brought them there, and parties of pirates were sent
out into the surrounding country to find the people
who had run away and to take from them the treasures they had carried off.    But although a great
many of the poor, miserable, unfortunate citizens
were captured and brought back to the town, there
was found upon them very little money, and but
few jewels or ornaments of value.    And now L'Olonnois began to prove how much worse his presence
was than any other misfortune which could have
happened to the town.    He tortured the poor prisoners, men, women, and children, to make them
tell where they had hidden their treasures, sometimes hacking one of them with his sword, declaring at the same time that if he did not tell where

his money was hidden he would immediately set to work to cut up his family and his friends.

The cruelties inflicted upon the inhabitants by this vile and beastly pirate and his men were so horrible that they could not be put into print. Even John Esquemeling, who wrote the account of it, had not the heart to tell everything that had happened. But after two weeks of horror and torture, the pirates were able to get but comparatively little out of the town, and they therefore determined to go somewhere else, where they might do better.

At the southern end of Lake Maracaibo, about forty leagues from the town which the pirates had just desolated and ruined, lay Gibraltar, a good-sized and prosperous town, and for this place L'Olonnois and his fleet now set sail; but they were not able to approach unsuspected and unseen, for news of their terrible doings had gone before them, and their coming was expected. When they drew near the town they saw the flag flying from the fort, and they knew that every preparation had been made for defence. To attack such a place as this was a rash undertaking; the Spaniards had perhaps a thousand soldiers, and the pirates numbered but three hundred and eighty, but L'Olonnois did not hesitate. As usual, he had no thought of bombardment, or any ordinary method of naval warfare; but at the first convenient spot he landed all his men, and having drawn them up in a body, he made them an address. He made them understand clearly the difficult piece of work which was before them ; but he assured them that pirates were so much in the habit of conquering Spaniards that if they would all promise to follow him and do their best, he was certain he could take the town. He assured them that it would be an ignoble thing to give up such a grand enterprise as this simply because they found the enemy strong and so well prepared to meet them, and ended by stating that if he saw a man flinch or hold back for a second, he would pistol him with his own hand. Whereupon the pirates all shook hands and promised they would follow L'Olonnois wherever he might lead them.

This they truly did, and L'Olonnois, having a very imperfect knowledge of the proper way to the town, led them into a wild bog, where this precious pack of rascals soon found themselves up to their knees in mud and water, and in spite of all the cursing and swearing which they did, they were not able to press through the bog or get out of it. In this plight they were discovered by a body of horsemen from the town, who began firing upon them. The Spaniards must now have thought that their game was almost bagged and that all they had to do was to stand on the edge of the bog and shoot down the floundering fellows who could not get

away from them.   But these fellows were bloody
buccaneers, each one of them a great deal harder
to kill than a cat, and they did not propose to stay
in the bog to be shot down.   With their cutlasses
they hewed off branches of trees and threw these
down in the bog, making a sort of rude roadway by
means of which they were able to get out on solid
ground.   But here they found themselves confronted by a large body of Spaniards, entrenched
behind earthworks.   Cannon and musket were
opened upon the buccaneers, and the noise and
smoke were so terrible they could scarcely hear the
commands of their leaders.

Never before, perhaps, had pirates been engaged
in such a land battle as this.   Very soon the Spaniards charged from behind their earthworks, and
then L'Olonnois and his men were actually obliged
to fly back.   If he could have found any way of
retreating to his ships, L'Olonnois would doubtless
have done so, in spite of his doughty words, when
he addressed his men, but this was now impossible,
for the Spaniards had felled trees and had made
a barricade between the pirates and their ships.
The buccaneers were now in a very tight place;
their enemy was behind defences and firing at them
steadily, without showing any intention of coming
out to give the pirates a chance for what they considered a fair fight.   Every now and then a buc-

caneer would fall, and L'Olonnois saw that as it would be utterly useless to endeavor to charge the barricade he must resort to some sort of trickery or else give up the battle.

Suddenly he passed the word for every man to turn his back and run away as fast as he could from the earthworks. Away scampered the pirates, and from the valiant Spaniards there came a shout of victory. The soldiers could not be restrained from following the fugitives and putting to death every one of the cowardly rascals. Away went the buccaneers, and after them, hot and furious, came the soldiers. But as soon as the Spaniards were so far away from their entrenchments that they could not get back to them, the crafty L'Olonnois, who ran with one eye turned behind him, called a halt, his men turned, formed into battle array, and began an onslaught upon their pursuing enemy, such as these military persons had never dreamed of in their wildest imagination. We are told that over two hundred Spaniards perished in a very short time. Before a furious pirate with a cutlass a soldier with his musket seemed to have no chance at all, and very soon the Spaniards who were left alive broke and ran into the woods.

The buccaneers formed into a body and marched toward the town, which surrendered without firing a gun, and L'Olonnois and his men, who, but an hour

before, had been in danger of being shot down by
their enemy as if they had been rabbits in a pen, now
marched boldly into the centre of the town, pulled
down the Spanish flag, and hoisted their own in its
place.    They were the masters of Gibraltar.    Never
had ambitious villany been more successful.

# Chapter XV

## A Just Reward

WHEN L'Olonnois and his buccaneers entered the town of Gibraltar they found that the greater part of the inhabitants had fled, but there were many people left, and these were made prisoners as fast as they were discovered. They were all forced to go into the great church, and then the pirates, fearing that the Spaniards outside of the town might be reënforced and come back again to attack them, carried a number of cannon into the church and fortified the building. When this had been done, they felt safe and began to act as if they had been a menagerie of wild beasts let loose upon a body of defenceless men, women, and children. Not only did these wretched men rush into the houses, stealing everything valuable they could find and were able to carry away, but when they had gathered together all they could discover they tortured their poor prisoners by every cruel method they could think of, in order to make them tell where more treasures were concealed. Many

of these unfortunates had had nothing to hide, and
therefore could give no information to their brutal
inquisitors, and others died without telling what
they had done with their valuables. When the
town had been thoroughly searched and sifted, the
pirates sent men out into the little villages and
plantations in the country, and even hunters and
small farmers were captured and made to give up
everything they possessed which was worth taking.

For nearly three weeks these outrageous proceedings continued, and to prove that they were lower
than the brute beasts they allowed the greater number of the prisoners collected in the church, to perish of hunger. There were not provisions enough
in the town for the pirates' own uses and for these
miserable creatures also, and so, with the exception
of a small quantity of mule flesh, which many of
the prisoners could not eat, they got nothing whatever, and slowly starved.

When L'Olonnois and his fiends had been in
possession of Gibraltar for about a month, they
thought it was time to leave, but their greedy souls
were not satisfied with the booty they had already
obtained, and they therefore sent messages to the
Spaniards who were still concealed in the forests,
that unless in the course of two days a ransom of
ten thousand pieces of eight were paid to them, they
would burn the town to the ground. No matter

what they thought of this heartless demand, it
was not easy for the scattered citizens to collect
such a sum as this, and the two days passed without
the payment of the ransom, and the relentless pirates
promptly carried out their threat and set the town
on fire in various places. When the poor Spaniards
saw this and perceived that they were about to lose
even their homes, they sent to the town and promised that if the pirates would put out the fires they
would pay the money. In the hope of more money,
and not in the least moved by any feeling of kindness, L'Olonnois ordered his men to help put out
the fires, but they were not extinguished until a
quarter of the town was entirely burned and a fine
church reduced to ashes.

When the buccaneers found they could squeeze
nothing more out of the town, they went on board
their ships, carrying with them all the plunder and
booty they had collected, and among their spoils
were about five hundred slaves, of all ages and both
sexes, who had been offered an opportunity to ransom themselves, but who, of course, had no money
with which to buy their freedom, and who were
now condemned to a captivity worse than anything
they had ever known before.

Now the eight ships with their demon crews sailed
away over the lake toward Maracaibo. It was
quite possible for them to get out to sea without

revisiting this unfortunate town, but as this would have been a very good thing for them to do, it was impossible for them to do it; no chance to do anything wicked was ever missed by these pirates. Consequently L'Olonnois gave orders to drop anchor near the city, and then he sent some messengers ashore to inform the already half-ruined citizens that unless they sent him thirty thousand pieces of eight he would enter their town again, carry away everything they had left, and burn the place to the ground. The poor citizens sent a committee to confer with the pirates, and while the negotiations were going on some of the conscienceless buccaneers went on shore and carried off from one of the great churches its images, pictures, and even its bells. It was at last arranged that the citizens should pay twenty thousand pieces of eight, which was the utmost sum they could possibly raise, and, in addition to this, five hundred head of beef-cattle, and the pirates promised that if this were done they would depart and molest the town no more. The money was paid, the cattle were put on board the ships, and to the unspeakable relief of the citizens, the pirate fleet sailed away from the harbor.

But it would be difficult to express the horror and dismay of those same citizens when, three days afterward, those pirate ships all came back again. Black despair now fell upon the town; there was nothing more to be stolen, and these wretches must have repented that they had left the town standing, and had returned to burn it down. But when one man came ashore in a boat bringing the intelligence that L'Olonnois could not get his largest ship across a bar at the entrance to the lake, and that he wanted a pilot to show him the channel, then the spirits of the people went up like one great united rocket, bursting into the most beautiful coruscations of sparks and colors. There was nothing on earth that they would be so glad to furnish him as a pilot to show him how to sail away from their shores. The pilot was instantly sent to the fleet, and L'Olonnois and his devastating band departed.

They did not go directly to Tortuga, but stopped at a little island near Hispaniola, which was inhabited by French buccaneers, and this delay was made entirely for the purpose of dividing the booty. It seems strange that any principle of right and justice should have been regarded by these dishonest knaves, even in their relations to each other, but they had rigid rules in regard to the division of their spoils, and according to these curious regulations the whole amount of plunder was apportioned among the officers and crews of the different ships.

Before the regular allotment of shares was made, the claims of the wounded were fully satisfied according to their established code. For the loss of a

right arm a man was paid about six hundred dollars,
or six slaves; for the loss of a left arm, five hundred
dollars, or five slaves; for a missing right leg, five
hundred dollars, or five slaves; for a missing left leg,
four hundred dollars, or four slaves; for an eye or a
finger, one hundred dollars, or one slave.    Then the
rest of the money and spoils were divided among all
the buccaneers without reference to what had been paid
to the wounded.   The shares of those who had been
killed were given to friends or acquaintances, who
undertook to deliver them to their families.

The spoils in this case consisted of two hundred
and sixty thousand dollars in money and a great
quantity of valuable goods, besides many slaves
and precious stones and jewels.   These latter were
apportioned among the men in the most ridiculous
manner, the pirates having no idea of the relative
value of the jewels, some of them preferring large
and worthless colored stones to smaller diamonds
and rubies.   When all their wickedly gained property had been divided, the pirates sailed to Tortuga,
where they proceeded, without loss of time, to get
rid of the wealth they had amassed.. They ate,
they drank, they gambled; they crowded the taverns as taverns have never been crowded before;
they sold their valuable merchandise for a twentieth
part of its value to some of the more level-headed
people of the place; and having rioted, gambled,

"The money and spoils were divided among all the buccaneers."
—p. 124.

and committed every sort of extravagance for about three weeks, the majority of L'Olonnois' rascally crew found themselves as poor as when they had started off on their expedition. It took them almost as long to divide their spoils as it did to get rid of them.

As these precious rascals had now nothing to live upon, it was necessary to start out again and commit some more acts of robbery and ruin; and L'Olonnois, whose rapacious mind seems to have been filled with a desire for town-destroying, projected an expedition to Nicaragua, where he proposed to pillage and devastate as many towns and villages as possible. His reputation as a successful commander was now so high that he had no trouble in getting men, for more offered themselves than he could possibly take.

He departed with seven hundred men and six ships, stopping on the way near the coast of Cuba, and robbing some poor fishermen of their boats, which he would need in shallow water. Their voyage was a very long one, and they were beset by calms, and instead of reaching Nicaragua, they drifted into the Gulf of Honduras. Here they found themselves nearly out of provisions, and were obliged to land and scour the country to find something to eat. Leaving their ships, they began a land march through the unfortunate region where they now found themselves. They robbed Indians, they robbed villages; they devastated little towns, taking everything that they cared for, and burning what they did not want, and treating the people they captured with viler cruelties than any in which the buccaneers had yet indulged. Their great object was to take everything they could find, and then try to make the people confess where other things were hidden. Men and women were hacked to pieces with swords; it was L'Olonnois' pleasure, when a poor victim had nothing to tell, to tear out his tongue with his own hands, and it is said that on some occasions his fury was so great that he would cut out the heart of a man and bite at it with his great teeth. No more dreadful miseries could be conceived than those inflicted upon the peaceful inhabitants of the country through which these wretches passed. They frequently met ambuscades of Spaniards, who endeavored to stop their progress; but this was impossible. The pirates were too strong in number and too savage in disposition to be resisted by ordinary Christians, and they kept on their wicked way.

At last they reached a town called San Pedro, which was fairly well defended, having around it a great hedge of prickly thorns; but thorns cannot keep out pirates, and after a severe fight the citizens surrendered, on condition that they should have two hours' truce. This was given, and the time was occupied by the people in running away into the woods and carrying off their valuables. But when the two hours had expired, L'Olonnois and his men entered the town, and instead of rummaging around to see what they could find, they followed the unfortunate people into the woods, for they well understood what they wanted when they asked for a truce, and robbed them of nearly everything they had taken away.

But the capture of this town was not of much service to L'Olonnois, who did not find provisions enough to feed his men. Their supplies ran very low, and it was not long before they were in danger of starvation. Consequently they made their way by the most direct course to the coast, where they hoped to be able to get something to eat. If they could find nothing else, they might at least catch fish. On their way every rascal of them prepared himself a net, made out of the fibres of a certain plant, which grew in abundance in those regions, in order that he might catch himself a supper when he reached the sea.

After a time the buccaneers got back to their fleet and remained on the coast about three months, waiting for some expected Spanish ships, which they hoped to capture. They eventually met with one, and after a great deal of ordinary fighting and stratagem they boarded and took her, but found her not a very valuable prize.

Now L'Olonnois proposed to his men that they should sail for Guatemala, but he met with an unexpected obstacle ; the buccaneers who had enlisted under him had expected to make great fortunes in this expedition, but their high hopes had not been realized. They had had very little booty and very little food, they were hungry and disappointed and wanted to go home, and the great majority of them declined to follow L'Olonnois any farther. But there were some who declared that they would rather die than go home to Tortuga as poor as when they left it, and so remained with L'Olonnois on the biggest ship of the fleet, which he commanded. The smaller vessels now departed for Tortuga, and after some trouble L'Olonnois succeeded in getting his vessel out of the harbor where it had been anchored, and sailed for the islands of de las Pertas. Here he had the misfortune to run his big vessel hopelessly aground.

When they found it absolutely impossible to get their great vessel off the sand banks, the pirates set to work to break her up and build a boat out of her planks. This was a serious undertaking, but it was all they could do. They could not swim away, and their ship was of no use to them as she was. But when they began to work they had no idea it would take so long to build a boat. It was several months before the unwieldy craft was finished, and they occupied part of the time in gardening, planting French beans, which came to maturity in six weeks, and gave them some fresh vegetables. They also had some stores and portable stoves on board their dismantled ship, and made bread from some wheat which was among their provisions, thus managing to live very well.

L'Olonnois was never intended by nature to be a boat-builder, or anything else that was useful and honest, and when the boat was finished it was discovered that it had been planned so badly that it would not hold them all, so all they could do was to draw lots to see who should embark in her, for one-half of them would have to stay until the others came back to release them. Of course L'Olonnois went away in the boat, and reached the mouth of the Nicaragua River. There his party was attacked by some Spaniards and Indians, who killed more than half of them and prevented the others from landing. L'Olonnois and the rest of his men got safely away, and they might now have sailed back to the island where they had left their comrades, for there was room enough for them all in the boat. But they did nothing of the sort, but went to the coast of Cartagena.

The pirates left on the island were eventually

taken off by a buccaneering vessel, but L'Olonnois
had now reached the end of the string by which the
devil had allowed him to gambol on this earth for
so long a time. On the shores where he had now
landed he did not find prosperous villages, treasure
houses, and peaceful inhabitants, who could be
robbed and tortured, but instead of these he came
upon a community of Indians, who were called by
the Spaniards, Bravos, or wild men. These people
would never have anything to do with the whites.
It was impossible to conquer them or to pacify
them by kind treatment. They hated the white
man and would have nothing to do with him.
They had heard of L'Olonnois and his buccaneers,
and when they found this notorious pirate upon their
shores they were filled with a fury such as they had
never felt for any others of his race.

These bloody pirates had always conquered in
their desperate fights because they were so reckless
and so savage, but now they had fallen among
thoroughbred savages, more cruel and more brutal
and pitiless than themselves. Nearly all the buccaneers were killed, and L'Olonnois was taken prisoner. His furious captors tore his living body
apart, piece by piece, and threw each fragment into
the fire, and when the whole of this most inhuman
of inhuman men had been entirely consumed, they
scattered his ashes to the winds so that not a trace

should remain on earth of this monster. If, in his infancy, he had died of croup, the history of the human race would have lost some of its blackest pages.

# Chapter XVI

## A Pirate Potentate

SOMETIME in the last half of the seventeenth century on a quiet farm in a secluded part of Wales there was born a little boy baby. His father was a farmer, and his mother churned, and tended the cows and the chickens, and there was no reason to imagine that this gentle little baby, born and reared in this rural solitude, would become one of the most formidable pirates that the world ever knew. Yet such was the case.

The baby's name was Henry Morgan, and as he grew to be a big boy a distaste for farming grew with him. So strong was his dislike that when he became a young man he ran away to the seacoast, for he had a fancy to be a sailor. There he found a ship bound for the West Indies, and in this he started out on his life's career. He had no money to pay his passage, and he therefore followed the usual custom of those days and sold himself for a term of three years to an agent who was taking out a number of men to work on the plantations. In the places where these men were enlisted they were termed servants, but when they got to the new world they were generally called slaves and treated as such.

When young Morgan reached the Barbadoes he was resold to a planter, and during his term of service he probably worked a good deal harder and was treated much more roughly than any of the laborers on his father's farm. But as soon as he was a free man he went to Jamaica, and there were few places in the world where a young man could be more free and more independent than in this lawless island.

Here were rollicking and blustering "flibustiers," and here the young man determined to study piracy. He was not a sailor and hunter who by the force of circumstances gradually became a buccaneer, but he deliberately selected his profession, and immediately set to work to acquire a knowledge of its practice. There was a buccaneer ship about to sail from Jamaica, and on this Morgan enlisted. He was a clever fellow and very soon showed himself to be a brave and able sailor.

After three or four voyages he acquired a reputation for remarkable coolness in emergencies, and showed an ability to take advantage of favorable circumstances, which was not possessed by many of his comrades. These prominent traits in his character became the foundation of his success. He

also proved himself a very good business man, and
having saved a considerable amount of money he
joined with some other buccaneers and bought a
ship, of which he took command. This ship soon
made itself a scourge in the Spanish seas; no other
buccaneering vessel was so widely known and so
greatly feared, and the English people in these
regions were as proud of the young Captain Morgan as if he had been a regularly commissioned
admiral, cruising against an acknowledged enemy.

Returning from one of his voyages Morgan found
an old buccaneer, named Mansvelt, in Jamaica, who
had gathered together a fleet of vessels with which
he was about to sail for the mainland. This expedition seemed a promising one to Morgan, and he
joined it, being elected vice-admiral of the fleet of
fifteen vessels. Since the successes of L'Olonnois
and others, attacks upon towns had become very
popular with the buccaneers, whose leaders were
getting to be tired of the retail branch of their business; that is, sailing about in one ship and capturing
such merchantmen as it might fall in with.

Mansvelt's expedition took with it not only six
hundred fighting pirates, but one writing pirate, for
John Esquemeling accompanied it, and so far as the
fame and reputation of these adventurers was concerned his pen was mightier than their swords, for
had it not been for his account of their deeds very

little about them would have been known to the world.

The fleet sailed directly for St. Catherine, an island near Costa Rica, which was strongly fortified by the Spaniards and used by them as a station for ammunition and supplies, and also as a prison. The pirates landed upon the island and made a most furious assault upon the fortifications, and although they were built of stone and well furnished with cannon, the savage assailants met with their usual good fortune. They swarmed over the walls and carried the place at the edge of the cutlass and the mouth of the pistol. In this fierce fight Morgan performed such feats of valor that even some of the Spaniards who had been taken prisoners, were forced to praise his extraordinary courage and ability as a leader.

The buccaneers proceeded to make very good use of their victory. They captured some small adjoining islands and brought the cannon from them to the main fortress, which they put in a good condition of defence. Here they confined all their prisoners and slaves, and supplied the island with an abundance of stores and provisions.

It is believed that when Mansvelt formed the plan of capturing this island he did so with the idea of founding there a permanent pirate principality, the inhabitants of which should not consider themselves English, French, or Dutch, but plain pirates, having a nationality and country of their own. Had the seed thus planted by Mansvelt and Morgan grown and matured, it is not unlikely that the whole of the West Indies might now be owned and inhabited by an independent nation, whose founders were the bold buccaneers.

When everything had been made tight and right at St. Catherine, Mansvelt and Morgan sailed for the mainland, for the purpose of attacking an inland town called Nata, but in this expedition they were not successful. The Spanish Governor of the province had heard of their approach, and met them with a body of soldiers so large that they prudently gave up the attempt, — a proceeding not very common with them, but Morgan was not only a dare-devil of a pirate, but a very shrewd Welshman.

They returned to the ships, and after touching at St. Catherine and leaving there enough men to defend it, under the command of a Frenchman named Le Sieur Simon, they sailed for Jamaica. Everything at St. Catherine was arranged for permanent occupation ; there was plenty of fresh water, and the ground could be cultivated, and Simon was promised that additional forces should be sent him so that he could hold the island as a regular station for the assembling and fitting out of pirate vessels.

The permanent pirate colony never came to anything; no reënforcements were sent; Mansvelt died, and the Spaniards gathered together a sufficient force to retake the island of St. Catherine, and make prisoners of Simon and his men. This was a blow to Morgan, who had had great hopes of the fortified station he thought he had so firmly established, but after the project failed he set about forming another expedition.

He was now recognized as buccaneer-in-chief of the West Indies, and he very soon gathered together twelve ships and seven hundred men. Everything was made ready to sail, and the only thing left to be done was to decide what particular place they should favor with a visit.

There were some who advised an attack upon Havana, giving as a reason that in that city there were a great many nuns, monks, and priests, and if they could capture them, they might ask as ransom for them, a sum a great deal larger than they could expect to get from the pillage of an ordinary town. But Havana was considered to be too strong a place for a profitable venture, and after several suggestions had been made, at last a deserter from the Spanish army, who had joined them, came forward with a good idea. He told the pirates of a town in Cuba, to which he knew the way; it was named Port-au-Prince, and was situated so far inland that it had never been sacked. When the pirates

heard that there existed an entirely fresh and unpil-
laged town, they were filled with as much excited
delight as if they had been a party of school-boys
who had just been told where they might find a
tree full of ripe apples which had been overlooked
by the men who had been gathering the crop.

When Morgan's fleet arrived at the nearest harbor to Port-au-Prince, he landed his men and
marched toward the town, but he did not succeed in
making a secret attack, as he had hoped. One of
his prisoners, a Spaniard, let himself drop overboard
as soon as the vessels cast anchor, and swimming
ashore, hurried to Port-au-Prince and informed the
Governor of the attack which was about to be made
on the town. Thus prepared, this able commander
knew just what to do. He marched a body of
soldiers along the road by which the pirates must
come, and when he found a suitable spot he caused
great trees to be cut down and laid across the road,
thus making a formidable barricade. Behind this
his soldiers were posted with their muskets and
their cannon, and when the pirates should arrive
they would find that they would have to do some
extraordinary fighting before they could pass this
well-defended barrier.

When Morgan came within sight of this barricade, he understood that the Spaniards had discovered his approach, and so he called a halt. He

had always been opposed to unnecessary work, and he considered that it would be entirely unnecessary to attempt to disturb this admirable defence, so he left the road, marched his men into the woods, led them entirely around the barricades, and then, after proceeding a considerable distance, emerged upon a wide plain which lay before the town. Here he found that he would have to fight his way into the city, and, probably much to his surprise, his men were presently charged by a body of cavalry.

Pirates, as a rule, have nothing to do with horses, either in peace or war, and the Governor of the town no doubt thought that when his well-armed horsemen charged upon these men, accustomed to fighting on the decks of ships, and totally unused to cavalry combats, he would soon scatter and disperse them. But pirates are peculiar fighters; if they had been attacked from above by means of balloons, or from below by mines and explosives, they would doubtless have adapted their style of defence to the method of attack. They always did this, and according to Esquemeling they nearly always got the better of their enemies; but we must remember that in cases where they did not succeed, as happened when they marched against the town of Nata, he says very little about the affair and amplifies only the accounts of their successes.

But the pirates routed the horsemen, and, after

a fight of about four hours, they routed all the other Spaniards who resisted them, and took possession of the town. Here they captured a great many prisoners which they shut up in the churches and then sent detachments out into the country to look for those who had run away. Then these utterly debased and cruel men began their usual course after capturing a town ; they pillaged, feasted, and rioted; they gave no thought to the needs of the prisoners whom they had shut up in the churches, many of whom starved to death; they tortured the poor people to make them tell where they had hid their treasures, and nothing was too vile or too wicked for them to do if they thought they could profit by it. They had come for the express purpose of taking everything that the people possessed, and until they had forced from them all that was of the slightest value, they were not satisfied. Even when the poor citizens seemed to have given up everything they owned they were informed that if they did not pay two heavy ransoms, one to protect themselves from being carried away into slavery, and one to keep their town from being burned, the same punishments would be inflicted upon them.

For two weeks the pirates waited for the unfortunate citizens to go out into the country and find some of their townsmen who had escaped with a portion of their treasure. In those days people did not keep their wealth in banks as they do now, but every man was the custodian of most of his own possessions, and when they fled from the visitation of an enemy they took with them everything of value that they could carry. If their fortunes had been deposited in banks, it would doubtless have been more convenient for the pirates.

Before the citizens returned Morgan made a discovery: a negro was captured who carried letters from the Governor of Santiago, a neighboring city, to some of the citizens of Port-au-Prince, telling them not to be in too great a hurry to pay the ransom demanded by the pirates, because he was coming with a strong force to their assistance. When Morgan read these letters, he changed his mind, and thought it would be a wise thing not to stay in that region any longer than could be helped. So he decided not to wait for the unfortunate citizens to collect the heavy ransom he demanded, but told them that if they would furnish him with five hundred head of cattle, and also supply salt and help prepare the meat for shipment, he would make no further demands upon them. This, of course, the citizens were glad enough to do, and when the buccaneers had carried to the ships everything they had stolen, and when the beef had been put on board, they sailed away.

Morgan directed the course of the fleet to a small island on which he wished to land in order that they might take an account of stock and divide the profits. This the pirates always did as soon as possible after they had concluded one of their nefarious enterprises. But his men were not at all satisfied with what happened on the island. Morgan estimated the total value of the booty to be about fifty thousand dollars, and when this comparatively small sum was divided, many of the men complained that it would not give them enough to pay their debts in Jamaica. They were utterly astonished that after having sacked an entirely fresh town they should have so little, and there is no doubt that many of them believed that their leader was a man who carried on the business of piracy for the purpose of enriching himself, while he gave his followers barely enough to keep them quiet.

There was, however, another cause of discontent among a large body of the men; it appears that the men were very fond of marrow-bones, and while they were yet at Port-au-Prince and the prisoners were salting the meat which was to go on the ships, the buccaneers went about among them and took the marrow-bones which they cooked and ate while they were fresh. One of the men, a Frenchman, had selected a very fine bone, and had put it by his side while he was preparing some other tidbits, when an Englishman came along, picked up the bone, and carried it away.

Now even in the chronicles of Mother Goose we are told of the intimate connection between Welshmen, thievery, and marrow-bones; for

> "Taffy was a Welshman,
> Taffy was a thief,
> Taffy came to my house
> And stole a leg of beef.

> "I went to Taffy's house,
> Taffy wasn't home,
> Taffy went to my house,
> And stole a marrow-bone."

What happened to Taffy we do not know, but Morgan was a Welshman, Morgan was a thief, and one of his men had stolen a marrow-bone; therefore came trouble. The Frenchman challenged the Englishman; but the latter, being a mean scoundrel, took advantage of his opponent, unfairly stabbed him in the back and killed him.

Now all the Frenchmen in the company rose in furious protest, and Morgan, wishing to pacify them, had the English assassin put in chains, and promised that he would take him to Jamaica and deliver him to justice. But the Frenchmen declined to be satisfied; they had received but very little money

after they had pillaged a rich town, and they believed that their English companions were inclined
to take advantage of them in every way, and consequently the greater part of them banded together
and deliberately deserted Morgan, who was obliged
to go back to Jamaica with not more than half his
regular forces, doubtless wishing that the cattle on
the island of Cuba had been able to get along without marrow-bones.

# Chapter XVII

## How Morgan was helped by Some Religious People

WHEN the Welsh buccaneer started out on another expedition his company consisted entirely of Englishmen, and was not nearly so large as it had been; when he announced to his followers that he intended to attack the fortified town of Porto Bello, on the mainland, there was a general murmuring among the men, for Porto Bello was one of the strongest towns possessed by the Spaniards, and the buccaneers did not believe that their comparatively small force would be able to take it. But Morgan made them a speech in which he endeavored to encourage them to follow him in this difficult undertaking. One of his arguments was, that although their numbers were small, their hearts were large; but he produced the greatest effect upon them when he said that as they were but a few, each man's share of the booty would be much larger than if it must be divided among a great number. This touched the souls of the

pirates, and they vowed to follow their leader where-
ever he might take them.

The buccaneers found Porto Bello a very hard nut
to crack ; they landed and marched upon the town,
which was defended by several forts or castles.
Even when one of these had been taken by assault,
and after it had been blown up with all its garrison,
who had been taken prisoners, still the town was
not intimidated, and the Governor vowed he would
never surrender, but would die fighting to the last.
The pirates raged like demons ; they shot down
every man they could see at the cannon or upon
the walls, and they made desperate efforts to capture
the principal fort, but they did not succeed, and
after a long time Morgan began to despair. The
garrison was strong and well commanded, and whenever the pirates attempted to scale the wall they
were shot down, while fire-pots full of powder,
with stones and other missiles, were hurled upon
them.

At last the wily Morgan had an idea. He set
his men to work to make some ladders high enough
to reach to the top of the walls, and wide enough to
allow three or four men to go up abreast. If he
could get these properly set up, his crew of desperate tiger-cats could make a combined rush and get
over the walls. But to carry the ladders and place
them would be almost impossible, for the men who

bore them would surely be shot down before they could finish the work. But it was not Morgan's plan that his men should carry these ladders. He had captured some convents in the suburbs of the town, with a number of nuns and monks, known as "religious people," and he now ordered these poor creatures, the women as well as the men, to take up the ladders and place them against the walls, believing that the Spanish Governor would not allow his soldiers to fire at these innocent persons whom the pirates had forced to do their will.

But the Governor was determined to defend the town no matter who had to suffer, and so the soldiers fired at the nuns and monks just as though they were buccaneers or any other enemies. The "religious people" cried out in terror, and screamed to their friends not to fire upon them; but the soldiers obeyed the commands of the Governor, while the pirates were swearing terribly behind them and threatening them with their pistols, and so the poor nuns and monks had to press forward, many of them dropping dead or wounded. They continued their work until the ladders were placed, and then over the walls went the pirates, with yells and howls of triumph, and not long after that the town was taken. The Governor died, fighting in the principal fort, and the citizens and soldiers all united in the most vigorous defence; but it was of no use.

Each pirate seemed to have not only nine lives, but nine arms, each one wielding a cutlass or aiming a pistol.

When the fighting was over, the second act in the horrible drama took place as usual. The pirates ate, drank, rioted, and committed all manner of outrages and cruelties upon the inhabitants, closing the performance with the customary threat that if the already distressed and impoverished inhabitants did not pay an enormous ransom, their town would be burned.

Before the ransom was paid, the Governor of Panama heard what was going on at Porto Bello, and sent a force to the assistance of the town, but this time the buccaneers did not hastily retreat. Morgan knew of a narrow defile through which the Spanish forces must pass, and there he posted a number of his men, who defended the pass so well that the Spaniards were obliged to retreat. This Governor must have been a student of military science; he was utterly astounded when he heard that this pirate leader, with less than four hundred men, had captured the redoubtable town of Porto Bello, defended by a strong garrison and inhabited by citizens who were brave and accustomed to fighting, and, being anxious to increase his knowledge of improved methods of warfare, he sent a messenger to Morgan " desiring him to send him some

small pattern of those arms wherewith he had taken
with such violence so great a city." The pirate
leader received the messenger with much courtesy,
and sent to the Governor a pistol and a few balls,
" desiring him to accept that slender pattern of the
arms wherewith he had taken Porto Bello, and
keep them for a twelvemonth; after which time he
promised to come to Panama and fetch them away."

This courteous correspondence was continued by
the Governor returning the pistol and balls with
thanks, and, also sending Morgan a handsome gold
ring with the message that he need not trouble himself to come to Panama; for, if he did, he would
meet with very different fortune from that which
had come to him at Porto Bello.

Morgan put the ring on his finger and postponed
his reply, and, as soon as the ransom was paid, he
put his booty on board his ships and departed.
When the spoils of Porto Bello came to be counted,
it was found that they were of great value, and each
man received a lordly share.

When Captain Morgan was ready to set out on
another expedition, he found plenty of pirates ready
to join him, and he commanded all the ships and
men whom he enlisted to rendezvous at a place
called the Isle of Cows. A fine, large, English
ship had recently come to Jamaica from New England, and this vessel also joined Morgan's forces on

the island, where the pirate leader took this ship as
his own, being much the best and largest vessel of
the fleet.

Besides the ships belonging to Morgan, there
was in the harbor where they were now congre-
gated, a fine vessel belonging to some French buccaneers, and Morgan desired very much that this
vessel should join his fleet, but the French cher-
ished hard feelings against the English, and would
not join them.

Although Morgan was a brave man, his meanness was quite equal to his courage, and he determined to be revenged upon these Frenchmen who
had refused to give him their aid, and therefore
played a malicious trick upon them. Sometime
before, this French vessel, being out of provisions
when upon the high seas, had met an English ship,
and had taken from her such supplies as it had
needed. The captain did not pay for these, being
out of money as well as food, not an uncommon
thing among buccaneers, but they gave the English
notes of exchange payable in Jamaica; but as these
notes were never honored, the people of the English
ship had never been paid for their provisions.

This affair properly arranged in Morgan's mind,
he sent a very polite note to the captain of the
French ship and some of his officers, inviting them
to dine with him on his own vessel. The French

"Morgan began to upbraid them, and ordered them taken below." —p. 151.

accepted the invitation, but when Morgan received them on board his ship he did not conduct them down to dinner; instead of that, he began to up-braid them for the manner in which they had treated an English crew, and then he ordered them to be taken down below and imprisoned in the hold. Having accomplished this, and feeling greatly elated by this piece of sly vengeance, he went into his fine cabin, and he and his officers sat down to the grand feast he had prepared.

There were fine times on board this great English ship; the pirates were about to set forth on an important expedition, and they celebrated the occasion by eating and drinking, firing guns, and all manner of riotous hilarity. In the midst of the wild fes-tivities — and nobody knew how it happened — a spark of fire got into the powder magazine, and the ship blew up, sending the lifeless bodies of three hundred English sailors, and the French prisoners, high into the air. The only persons on board who escaped were Morgan and his officers who were in the cabin close to the stern of the vessel, at some distance from the magazine.

This terrible accident threw the pirate fleet into great confusion for a time; but Morgan soon recov-ered himself, and, casting about to see what was the best thing to be done, it came into his head that he would act the part of the wolf in the fable of the wolf and the lamb. As there was no way of finding out how the magazine happened to explode, he took the ground that the French prisoners whom he had shut up in the hold, had thrown a lighted match into the magazine, wishing thus to revenge themselves even though they should, at the same time, lose their own lives. The people of the French ship bitterly opposed any such view of the case, but their protestations were of no use; they might declare as much as they pleased that it was impossible for them to make the waters muddy, being lower down in the stream than the wolfish pirate who was accusing them, but it availed nothing. Morgan sprang upon them and their ship, and sent them to Jamaica, where, upon his false charge, they were shut up in prison, and so remained for a long time.

Such atrocious wickedness as the treatment of the nuns and monks, described in this chapter, would never have been countenanced in any warfare between civilized nations. But Morgan's pirates were not making war; they were robbers and murderers on a grand scale. They had no right to call themselves civilized; they were worse than barbarians.

# Chapter XVIII

## A Piratical Aftermath

MORGAN'S destination was the isle of Savona, near which a great Spanish fleet was expected to pass, and here he hoped to make some rich prizes. But when he got out to sea he met with contrary and dangerous winds, which delayed him a long time, and eventually when he arrived at Savona, after having landed at various places, where he pillaged, murdered, and. burned, according to the extent of his opportunities, he found at least one-half of his men and ships had not arrived. With the small force which he now had with him he could not set out to attack a Spanish fleet, and therefore he was glad to accept the suggestion made to him by a Frenchman who happened to be in his company.

This man had been with L'Olonnois two years before when that bloody pirate had sacked the towns of Maracaibo and Gibraltar; he had made himself perfectly familiar with the fortifications and defences of these towns, and he told Morgan that it would

be easy to take them. To be sure they had been
thoroughly sacked before, and therefore did not offer
the tempting inducements of perfectly fresh towns,
such as Port-au-Prince, but still in two years the
inhabitants must have gathered together some possessions desirable to pirates, and therefore, although
Morgan could not go to these towns with the
expectation of reaping a full harvest, he might at
least gather up an aftermath which would pay him
for his trouble.

So away sailed this horde of ravenous scoundrels
for the lake of Maracaibo, at the outer end of which
lay the town of Maracaibo, and at the other ex-
tremity the town of Gibraltar. When they had
sailed near enough to the fortifications they anchored
out of sight of the watch-tower and, landing in the
night, marched on one of the forts. Here the
career of Morgan came very near closing forever.
The Spaniards had discovered the approach of the
pirates, and this fort had been converted into a
great trap in which the citizens hoped to capture
and destroy the pirate leader and his men. Everybody had left the fort, the gates were open, and a
slow-match, communicating with the magazine,
had been lighted just before the last Spaniard
had left.

But the oldest and most sagacious of rats would
be no more difficult to entrap than was the wily

pirate Morgan. When he entered the open gates of the fort and found everything in perfect order, he suspected a trick, and looking about him he soon saw the smouldering match. Instantly he made a dash at it, seized it and extinguished the fire. Had he been delayed in this discovery a quarter of an hour longer, he and his men would have been blown to pieces along with the fort.

Now the pirates pressed on toward the town, but they met with no resistance. The Spaniards, having failed to blow up their dreaded enemies, had retreated into the surrounding country and had left the town. The triumphant pirates spread themselves everywhere. They searched the abandoned town for people and valuables, and every man who cared to do so took one of the empty houses for his private residence. They made the church the common meeting-place where they might all gather together when it was necessary, and when they had spent the night in eating and drinking all the good things they could find, they set out the next day to hunt for the fugitive citizens.

For three weeks Morgan and his men held a devil's carnival in Maracaibo. To tell of the abominable tortures and cruelties which they inflicted upon the poor people, whom they dragged from their hiding-places in the surrounding country, would make our flesh creep and our blood run cold.

When they could do no more evil they sailed away up the lake for Gibraltar.

It is not necessary to tell the story of the taking of this town. When Morgan arrived there he found it also entirely deserted. The awful dread of the human beasts who were coming upon them had forced the inhabitants to fly. In the whole town only one man was left, and he was an idiot who had not sense enough to run away. This poor fellow was tortured to tell where his treasures were hid, and when he consented to take them to the place where he had concealed his possessions, they found a few broken earthen dishes, and a little bit of money, about as much as a poor imbecile might be supposed to possess. Thereupon the disappointed fiends cruelly killed him.

For five weeks the country surrounding Gibraltar was the scene of a series of diabolical horrors. The pirates undertook the most hazardous and difficult expeditions in order to find the people who had hidden themselves on islands and in the mountains, and although they obtained a great deal of booty, they met with a good many misfortunes. Some of them were drowned in swollen streams, and others lost much of their pillage by rains and storms.

At last, after having closed his vile proceedings in the ordinary pirate fashion, by threatening to burn the town if he were not paid a ransom, Morgan

thought it time for him to depart, for if the Spaniards should collect a sufficient force at Maracaibo
to keep him from getting out of the lake, he would
indeed be caught in a trap. The ransom was partly
paid and partly promised, and Morgan and his men
departed, carrying with them some hostages for the
rest of the ransom due.

When Morgan and his fleet arrived at Maracaibo,
they found the town still deserted, but they also
discovered that they were caught in the trap which
they had feared, out of which they saw no way of
escaping. News had been sent the Spanish forces
of the capture and sacking of Maracaibo, and three
large men-of-war now lay in the channel below the
town which led from the lake into the sea. And
more than this, the castle which defended the entrance to the lake, and which the pirates had found
empty when they arrived, was now well manned
and supplied with a great many cannon, so that for
once in their lives these wicked buccaneers were
almost discouraged. Their little ships could not
stand against the men-of-war; and in any case they
could not pass the castle, which was now prepared
to blow them to pieces if they should come near
enough.

But in the midst of these disheartening circumstances, the pirate leader showed what an arrogant,
blustering dare-devil he was, for, instead of admitting

his discomfiture and trying to make terms with the
Spaniards, he sent a letter to the admiral of the
ships, in which he stated that if he did not allow
him a free passage out to sea he would burn every
house in Maracaibo. To this insolent threat, the
Spanish admiral replied in a long letter, in which
he told Morgan that if he attempted to leave the
lake he would fire upon his ships, and, if necessary,
follow them out to sea, until not a stick of one of
them should be left. But in the great magnanimity
of his soul he declared that he would allow Morgan
to sail away freely, provided he would deliver all the
booty he had captured, together with the prisoners
and slaves, and promise to go home and abandon
buccaneering forever. In case he declined these
terms, the admiral declared he would come up the
channel in boats filled with his soldiers and put
every pirate to the sword.

When Morgan received this letter, he called his
men together in the public square of the town, and
asked them what they would do, and when these
fellows heard that they were asked to give up all
their booty, they unanimously voted that they
would perish rather than do such an unmanly thing
as that. So it was agreed that they would fight
themselves out of the lake of Maracaibo, or stay
there, dead or alive, as the case might be.

# Chapter XIX

## A Tight Place for Morgan

AT this important crisis again turned up the man with an idea. This was an inventive buccaneer, who proposed to Morgan that they should take a medium-sized ship which they had captured at the other end of the lake, and make a fire-ship of her. In order that the Spaniards might not suspect the character of this incendiary craft, he proposed that they should fit her up like one of the pirate war-vessels, for in this case the Spaniards would not try to get away from her, but would be glad to have her come near enough for them to capture her.

Morgan was pleased with this plan, and the fire-ship was prepared with all haste. All the pitch, tar, and brimstone in the town were put on board of her, together with other combustibles. On the deck were placed logs of wood, which were dressed up in coats and hats to look like men, and by their sides were muskets and cutlasses. Portholes were made, and in these were placed other logs to represent cannon. Thus this merchant vessel, now as inflammable as a pine knot, was made to resemble a somewhat formidable pirate ship. The rest of the fleet was made ready, the valuables and prisoners and slaves were put on board; and they all sailed boldly down toward the Spanish vessels, the fire-ship in front.

When the Spanish admiral saw this insignificant fleet approaching, he made ready to sink it to the bottom, and when the leading vessel made its way directly toward his own ship, as if with the impudent intention of boarding her, he did not fire at her, but let her come on. The few pirates on board the fire-ship ran her up against the side of the great man-of-war; and after making her fast and applying their matches, they immediately slipped overboard, and swam to one of their own vessels before the Spaniards had an idea of what had happened. The fire-ship was soon ablaze, and as the flames quickly spread, the large vessel took fire, and the people on board had scarcely time to get out of her before she sank.

The commander of one of the other ships was so much frightened by what had occurred in so short a space of time that he ran his vessel aground and wrecked her, her men jumping out into the water and making for the land. As for the other ship, the pirates boldly attacked her and captured her, and as she was a very fine vessel, Morgan left his own small vessel, in which he had been commanding his fleet, and took possession of her. Thus, in a very short time, the whole state of affairs was changed. The Spaniards had no ships at all, and Morgan was in command of a very fine vessel, in which he led his triumphant fleet.

Victory is a grand thing to a pirate as it is to every human being who has been engaged in a conflict, but none of the joys of triumph could equal the sordid rapacity of Morgan and his men. They spent days in trying to recover the money and plate which were on board the sunken Spanish ships. The sterns of these projected above water, and a great deal of valuable treasure was recovered from them. The pirates worked very hard at this, although they had not the slightest idea how they were to pass the castle and get away with the plunder after they had obtained it.

When the wrecks had been stripped of everything of value, the time came for demanding a ransom for not burning the town and hanging the prisoners, and as the poor citizens knew very well what they might expect, they sent word to the admiral, who had escaped to the castle, begging him to accede to the demands of Morgan, and to let the wretched pirates go. But the admiral, Don Alonso, was a thoroughbred Spaniard, and he would listen to no

such cowardly suggestion. He would consent to
no ransom being paid, and on no account would he
allow the pirates to pass the channel. The citizens,
however, who knew what was good for them, raised
the money, and paid the ransom in coin and cattle,
and Morgan declared that if the admiral would not
let him out of the lake, he would have to attend to
that matter himself.

But before he made another bold stroke against
the enemy his stingy and niggardly spirit urged
him to defend himself against his friends, and before endeavoring to leave he ordered a division of
the spoils. Many of the goods taken from the two
towns were on board the different vessels of the
fleet, and he was very much afraid that if his comrades, who commanded the other ships, should be
so fortunate as to get out to sea, they would sail
away with the booty they carried, and he would not
see any of it. Therefore, the booty from every
ship was brought on board his own fine vessel, and
every man was put through an examination as rigid
as if he had been passing a custom house, and was
obliged to prove that he had not concealed or kept
back any money or jewels. The value of the plunder was very great, and when it had been divided,
according to the scale which Morgan had adopted,
the pirate leader felt safe. He now had his
share of the prizes in his own possession, and

that to him was more important than anything else in the world.

The question of getting away was a very serious one; the greater part of his fleet consisted of small vessels which could not defy the guns of the fort, and as the stout hearts and brawny arms of his followers could be of no use to him in this dilemma, Morgan was obliged to fall back upon his own brains; therefore, he planned a trick.

When everything had been prepared for departure, Morgan anchored his fleet at a distance from the castle, but not so far away that the Spaniards could not observe his movements. Then he loaded some boats with armed men and had them rowed ashore on the side of the channel on which the castle stood. The boats landed behind a little wood, and there the men, instead of getting out, crouched themselves down in the bottom of the boats so that they should not be seen. Then the boats, apparently empty, were rowed back to the pirate ships, and in a short time, again full of men sitting upright, with their muskets and cutlasses, they went to the shore, and soon afterwards returned apparently empty as before.

This performance was repeated over and over again, until the people in the castle were convinced that Morgan was putting his men on shore in order to make a land attack upon the rear of the castle

during the night. But the Spanish admiral was
not to be caught by any such clumsy stratagem as
that, and, therefore, in great haste he had his big
cannon moved to the land side of the fort, and
posted there the greater part of his garrison in
order that when the pirates made their assault in
the dead of the night they would meet with a reception for which they had not bargained.

When it was dark, and the tide began to run
out, the pirate vessels weighed anchor, and they
all drifted down toward the castle. Morgan's spies
had perceived some of the extraordinary movements
in the Spanish fortifications, and he therefore drifted
down with a good deal of confidence, although, had
his trick been discovered in time it would have gone
very hard with his fleet. It is probable that he had
taken all these chances into consideration and had
felt pretty sure that if the cannon of the fort had
been opened upon them it would not have been the
big ship which carried him and his precious load
which would have been sunk by the great guns, and
that no matter what happened to the smaller vessels
and the men on board them, he and his own ship
would be able to sail away.

But the Spaniards did not perceive the approach
of the drifting fleet, for they were intrepidly waiting
at the back of the castle to make it very hot for the
pirates when they should arrive. Slowly past the

great walls of the fort drifted the fleet of buccaneers, and then, at a signal, every vessel hoisted its sails, and, with a good wind, sailed rapidly toward the open sea. The last pirate vessel had scarcely passed the fort when the Spaniards discovered what was going on, and in great haste they rolled their cannon back to the water side of the fort and began firing furiously, but it was of no use.

The pirates sailed on until they were out of danger, and then they anchored and arranged for putting on shore the greater number of their prisoners, who were only an encumbrance to them. As a parting insult, Morgan fired seven or eight of his largest guns at the castle, whose humiliated occupants did not reply by a single shot.

In order to understand what thoroughly contemptible scoundrels these pirates were it may be stated that when Morgan and his men reached Jamaica after a good deal of storm and trouble on the way, they found there many of their comrades who had not been able to join them at their rendezvous at Savona. These unfortunate fellows, who had not known where Morgan had gone and were unable to join him, had endeavored to do some piratical business of their own, but had had very little luck and a great many misfortunes. Morgan's men, with their pockets full of money, jeered and sneered at their poor comrades who had had such hard times, and without any thought of sharing with them the least portion of their own vile gains they treated them with contempt and derision.

The buccaneer, Captain Henry Morgan, was now a very great personage, but with his next expedition, which was a very important one, and in its extent resembled warfare rather than piracy, we shall have little to do because his exploits in this case were not performed on our Atlantic coasts, but over the Isthmus, on the shores of the Pacific.

Morgan raised a great fleet, carrying a little army of two thousand men, and with this he made his way to the other side of the Isthmus and attacked the city of Panama, which, of course, he captured. His terrible deeds at this place resembled those which he performed after the capture of the smaller towns which we have been considering, except that they were on a scale of greater magnitude. Nearly the whole of the town of Panama was burned, and the excesses, cruelties, and pillages of the conquerors were something almost without parallel.

Before marching overland to Panama, Morgan had recaptured the island of St. Catherine, which was a very valuable station for his purposes, and had also taken the castle of Chagres on the mainland near by, and on his return from the conquest and pillage of the unfortunate city he and his forces gathered together at Chagres in order to divide the spoils.

Now came great trouble and dissatisfaction; many of the buccaneers loudly declared that Morgan was taking everything that was really valuable for his own, especially the precious stones and jewels, and that they were getting a very small share of the booty of Panama. There seemed to be good reason for these complaints, for the sum of about two hundred dollars apiece was all that Morgan's men received after their terrible hardships and dangers and the pillage of a very rich town. The murmurings and complaints against Morgan's peculiar methods became louder and more frequent, and at last the wily Welshman began to be afraid that serious trouble would come to him if he did not take care of himself. This, however, he was very capable of doing. Silently and quietly one night, without giving notice to any of the buccaneers at Chagres, except a few who were in his secret, Morgan, in his large ship, sailed away for Jamaica, followed by only a few other vessels, containing some of his favored companions.

When the great body of the buccaneers, the principal portion of which were Frenchmen, found that their leader had deserted them, there was a grand commotion, and if they had been able, the furious men who had had this trick played upon them, would have followed Morgan to treat him as they had so often treated the Spaniards. But they could not follow— Morgan had taken great care that this should not happen. Their ships were out of order; they had been left very short of provisions and ammunition, and found that not only were they unable to avenge themselves on their traitor leader, but that it would be very hard for them to get away at all.

Poor Esquemeling, the literary pirate, was one of those who was left behind, and in his doleful state he made the following reflection, which we quote from his book: "Captain Morgan left us all in such a miserable condition as might serve for a lively representation of what rewards attend wickedness at the latter end of life. Whence we ought to have learned how to regulate and amend our actions for the future."

After Morgan had safely reached Jamaica with all his booty, the idea renewed itself in his mind of returning to St. Catherine, fortifying the place and putting it in complete order, and then occupying it as a station for all pirates, with himself the supreme governor and king of the buccaneers. But before he had completed his arrangements for doing this there was a change in the affairs at Jamaica: the king of England, having listened to the complaints of the Spanish crown, had recalled the former Governor and put him on trial to answer for the manner in which he allowed the island to be used by the pirates for their wicked purposes against a friendly nation, and had sent a new Governor with orders to allow no buccaneers in Jamaica, and in every way to suppress piracy in those parts.

Now the shrewd Morgan saw that his present business was likely to become a very undesirable one, and he accordingly determined to give it up. Having brutally pillaged and most cruelly treated the Spaniards as long as he was able to do so, and having cheated and defrauded his friends and companions to the utmost extent possible, he made up his mind to reform, and a more thoroughly base and contemptible reformed scoundrel was never seen on the face of the earth.

Morgan was now a rich man, and he lost no time in becoming very respectable. He endeavored to win favor with the new Governor, and was so successful that when that official was obliged to return to England on account of his health, he left the ex-pirate in charge of the affairs of the island in the capacity of Deputy-Governor. More than this, King Charles, who apparently had heard of Morgan's great bravery and ability, and had not cared to listen to anything else about him, knighted him, and this preëminent and inhuman water-thief became Sir Henry Morgan.

In his new official capacity Morgan was very severe upon his former associates, and when any of them were captured and brought before him, he

condemned some to be imprisoned and some to be
hung, and in every way apparently endeavored to
break up the unlawful business of buccaneering.

About this time John Esquemeling betook himself to Europe with all possible despatch, for he had
work to do and things to tell with which the Deputy-
Governor would have no sympathy whatever. He
got away safely, and he wrote his book, and if he
had not had this good fortune, the world would have
lost a great part of the story of what happened to
the soft little baby who was born among the quiet
green fields of Wales.

Even during the time that he was Deputy-Governor, Morgan was suspected of sharing in the gains
of some buccaneers at the same time that he pun-
ished others, and after the death of Charles II. he
was sent to England and imprisoned, but what
eventually became of him we do not know. If he
succeeded in ill-using and defrauding his Satanic
Majesty, there is no record of the fact.

# Chapter XX

## The Story of a High-Minded Pirate

AFTER having considered the extraordinary performances of so many of those execrable wretches, the buccaneers, it is refreshing and satisfactory to find that there were exceptions even to the rules which governed the conduct and general make-up of the ordinary pirate of the period, and we are therefore glad enough to tell the story of a man, who, although he was an out-and-out buccaneer, possessed some peculiar characteristics which give him a place of his own in the history of piracy.

In the early part of these sketches we have alluded to a gentleman of France, who, having become deeply involved in debt, could see no way of putting himself in a condition to pay his creditors but to go into business of some kind. He had no mercantile education, he had not learned any profession, and it was therefore necessary for him to do something for which a previous preparation was not absolutely essential.

After having carefully considered all the methods

of making money which were open to him under the
circumstances, he finally concluded to take up piracy
and literature.   Even at the present day it is considered by many persons that one of these branches
of industry is a field of action especially adapted to
those who have not had the opportunity of giving
the time and study necessary in any other method
of making a living.

The French gentleman whose adventures we are
about to relate was a very different man from John
Esquemeling, who was a literary pirate and nothing
more.   Being of a clerkly disposition, the gentle
John did not pretend to use the sabre or the pistol.
His part in life was simply to watch his companions
fight, burn, and steal, while his only weapon was his
pen, with which he set down their exploits and
thereby murdered their reputations.

But Monsieur Raveneau de Lussan was both
buccaneer and author, and when he had finished his
piratical career he wrote a book in which he gave a
full account of it, thus showing that although he had
not been brought up to a business life, he had very
good ideas about money-making.

More than that, he had very good ideas about
his own reputation, and instead of leaving his exploits
and adventures to be written up by other people, —
that is, if any one should think it worth while to do
so, — he took that business into his own hands.

He was well educated, he had been brought up in good society, and as he desired to return to that society it was natural for him to wish to paint his own portrait as a buccaneer. Pictures of that kind as they were ordinarily executed were not at all agreeable to the eyes of the cultivated classes of France, and so M. de Lussan determined to give his personal attention not only to his business speculations, but to his reputation. He went out as a buccaneer in order to rob the Spaniards of treasure with which to pay his honest debts, and, in order to prevent his piratical career being described in the coarse and disagreeable fashion in which people generally wrote about pirates, he determined to write his own adventures.

If a man wishes to appear well before the world, it is often a very good thing for him to write his autobiography, especially if there is anything a little shady in his career, and it may be that de Lussan's reputation as a high-minded pirate depends somewhat on the book he wrote after he had put down the sword and taken up the pen; but if he gave a more pleasing color to his proceedings than they really deserved, we ought to be glad of it. For, even if de Lussan the buccaneer was in some degree a creature of the imagination of de Lussan the author, we have a story which is much more pleasing and, in some respects, more romantic than stories of ordinary pirates could possibly be made unless the writer of such stories abandoned fact altogether and plunged blindly into fiction.

Among the good qualities of de Lussan was a pious disposition. He had always been a religious person, and, being a Catholic, he had a high regard and veneration for religious buildings, for priests, and for the services of the church, and when he had crossed the Atlantic in his ship, the crew of which was composed of desperadoes of various nations, and when he had landed upon the western continent, he wished still to conform to the religious manners and customs of the old world.

Having a strong force under his command and possessing, in common with most of the gentlemen of that period, a good military education, it was not long after he landed on the mainland before he captured a small town. The resistance which he met was soon overcome, and our high-minded pirate found himself in the position of a conqueror with a community at his mercy. As his piety now raised itself above all his other attributes, the first thing that he did was to repair to the principal church of the town, accompanied by all his men, and here, in accordance with his commands, a Te Deum was sung and services were conducted by the priests in charge. Then, after having properly performed his religious duties, de Lussan sent his men through the town with orders to rob the inhabitants of everything valuable they possessed.

The ransacking and pillaging of the houses continued for some time, but when the last of his men had returned with the booty they had collected, the high-minded chief was dissatisfied. The town appeared to be a good deal poorer than he had expected, and as the collection seemed to be so very small, de Lussan concluded that in some way or other he must pass around the hat again. While he was wondering how he should do this he happened to hear that on a sugar plantation not very far away from the town there were some ladies of rank who, having heard of the approach of the pirates, had taken refuge there, thinking that even if the town should be captured, their savage enemies would not wander into the country to look for spoils and victims.

But these ladies were greatly mistaken. When de Lussan heard where they were, he sent out a body of men to make them prisoners and bring them back to him. They might not have any money or jewels in their possession, but as they belonged to good families who were probably wealthy, a good deal of money could be made out of them by holding them and demanding a heavy ransom for their release. So the ladies were all brought to town and shut up securely until their

friends and relatives managed to raise enough money
to pay their ransom and set them free, and then, I
have no doubt, de Lussan advised them to go to
church and offer up thanks for their happy deliverance.

As our high-minded pirate pursued his plunder-
ing way along the coast of South America, he met
with a good many things which jarred upon his sensitive nature — things he had not expected when he
started out on his new career.  One of his disappointments was occasioned by the manners and customs of the English buccaneers under his command.
These were very different from the Frenchmen of
his company, for they made not the slightest pretence to piety.

When they had captured a town or a village, the
Englishmen would go to the churches, tear down
the paintings, chop the ornaments from the altars
with their cutlasses, and steal the silver crucifixes,
the candlesticks, and even the communion services.
Such conduct gave great pain to de Lussan.  To
rob and destroy the property of churches was in his
eyes a great sin, and he never suffered anything of
the kind if he could prevent it.  When he found in
any place which he captured a wealthy religious
community or a richly furnished church, he scrupu-
lously refrained from taking anything or of doing
damage to property, and contented himself with

demanding heavy indemnity, which the priests were obliged to pay as a return for the pious exemption which he granted them.

But it was very difficult to control the Englishmen. They would rob and destroy a church as willingly as if it were the home of a peaceful family, and although their conscientious commander did everything he could to prevent their excesses, he did not always succeed. If he had known what was likely to happen, his party would have consisted entirely of Frenchmen.

Another thing which disappointed and annoyed the gentlemanly de Lussan was the estimation in which the buccaneers were held by the ladies of the country through which he was passing. He soon found that the women in the Spanish settlements had the most horrible ideas regarding the members of the famous " Brotherhood of the Coast." To be sure, all the Spanish settlers, and a great part of the natives of the country, were filled with horror and dismay whenever they heard that a company of buccaneers was within a hundred miles of their homes, and it is not surprising that this was the case, for the stories of the atrocities and cruelties of these desperadoes had spread over the western world.

But the women of the settlements looked upon the buccaneers with greater fear and abhorrence than

the men could possibly feel, for the belief was almost
universal among them that buccaneers were terrible
monsters of cannibal habits who delighted in devour-
ing human beings, especially if they happened to
be young and tender. This ignorance of the true
character of the invaders of the country was greatly
deplored by de Lussan. He had a most profound
pity for those simple-minded persons who had allowed themselves to be so deceived in regard to the
real character of himself and his men, and whenever he had an opportunity, he endeavored to persuade the ladies who fell in his way that sooner
than eat a woman he would entirely abstain from
food.

On one occasion, when politely conducting a
young lady to a place of confinement, where in
company with other women of good family she was
to be shut up until their relatives could pay handsome ransoms for their release, he was very much
surprised when she suddenly turned to him with
tears in her eyes, and besought him not to devour
her. This astonishing speech so wounded the feelings of the gallant Frenchman that for a moment
he could not reply, and when he asked her what
had put such an unreasonable fear in her mind,
she could only answer that she thought he looked
hungry, and that perhaps he would not be willing to
wait until — And there she stopped, for she could

not bring her mind to say — until she was properly prepared for the table.

"What!" exclaimed the high-minded pirate. "Do you suppose that I would eat you in the street?" And as the poor girl, who was now crying, would make him no answer, he fell into a sombre silence which continued until they had reached their destination.

The cruel aspersions which were cast upon his character by the women of the country were very galling to the chivalrous soul of this gentleman of France, and in every way possible he endeavored to show the Spanish ladies that their opinions of him were entirely incorrect, and even if his men were rather a hard lot of fellows, they were not cannibals.

The high-minded pirate had now two principal objects before him. One was to lay his hand upon all the treasure he could find, and the other was to show the people of the country, especially the ladies, that he was a gentleman of agreeable manners and a pious turn of mind.

It is highly probable that for some time the hero of this story did not succeed in his first object as well as he would have liked. A great deal of treasure was secured, but some of it consisted of property which could not be easily turned into cash or carried away, and he had with him a body of rapacious and conscienceless scoundrels who were

continually clamoring for as large a share of the
available spoils — such as jewels, money, and small
articles of value — as they could induce their commander to allow them, and, in consequence of this
greediness of his own men, his share of the plunder
was not always as large as it ought to be.

But in his other object he was very much more
successful, and, in proof of this, we have only to relate an interesting and remarkable adventure which
befell him.    He laid siege to a large town, and, as
the place was well defended by fortifications and
armed men, a severe battle took place before it was
captured.    But at last the town was taken, and
de Lussan and his men having gone to church to
give thanks for their victory, — his Englishmen
being obliged to attend the services no matter what
they did afterward, — he went diligently to work to
gather from the citizens their valuable and available
possessions.    In this way he was brought into personal contact with a great many of the people of the
town, and among the acquaintances which he made
was that of a young Spanish lady of great beauty.

The conditions and circumstances in the midst of
which this lady found herself after the city had been
taken, were very peculiar.    She had been the wife
of one of the principal citizens, the treasurer of the
town, who was possessed of a large fortune, and who
lived in one of the best houses in the place ; but

during the battle with the buccaneers, her husband, who fought bravely in defence of the place, was killed, and she now found herself not only a widow, but a prisoner in the hands of those ruthless pirates whose very name had struck terror into the hearts of the Spanish settlers. Plunged into misery and despair, it was impossible for her to foresee what was going to happen to her.

As has been said, the religious services in the church were immediately followed by the pillage of the town ; every house was visited, and the trembling inhabitants were obliged to deliver up their treasures to the savage fellows who tramped through their halls and rooms, swearing savagely when they did not find as much as they expected, and laughing with wild glee at any unusual discovery of jewels or coin.

The buccaneer officers as well as the men assisted in gathering in the spoils of the town, and it so happened that M. Raveneau de Lussan, with his good clothes and his jaunty hat with a feather in it, selected the house of the late treasurer of the city as a suitable place for him to make his investigations. He found there a great many valuable articles and also found the beautiful young widow.

The effect produced upon the mind of the lady when the captain of the buccaneers entered her house was a very surprising one. Instead of beholding a savage, brutal ruffian, with ragged clothes and gleaming teeth, she saw a handsome gentleman, as well dressed as circumstances would permit, very polite in his manners, and with as great a desire to transact his business without giving her any more inconvenience than was necessary, as if he had been a tax-collector or had come to examine the gas meter. If all the buccaneers were such agreeable men as this one, she and her friends had been laboring under a great mistake.

De Lussan did not complete his examination of the treasurer's house in one visit, and during the next two or three days the young widow not only became acquainted with the character of buccaneers in general, but she learned to know this particular buccaneer very well, and to find out what an entirely different man he was from the savage fellows who composed his company. She was grateful to him for his kind manner of appropriating her possessions, she was greatly interested in his society, — for he was a man of culture and information, — and in less than three days she found herself very much in love with him. There was not a man in the whole town who, in her opinion, could compare with this gallant commander of buccaneers.

It was not very long before de Lussan became conscious of the favor he had found in the eyes of this lady; for as a buccaneer could not be expected to remain very long in one place, it was necessary, if this lady wished the captor of her money and treasure to know that he had also captured her heart, that she must not be slow in letting him know the state of her affections, and being a young person of a very practical mind she promptly informed de Lussan that she loved him and desired him to marry her.

The gallant Frenchman was very much amazed when this proposition was made to him, which was in the highest degree complimentary. It was very attractive to him — but he could not understand it. The lady's husband had been dead but a few days — he had assisted in having the unfortunate gentleman properly buried — and it seemed to him very unnatural that the young widow should be in such an extraordinary hurry to prepare a marriage feast before the funeral baked meats had been cleared from the table.

There was but one way in which he could explain to himself this remarkable transition from grief to a new affection. He believed that the people of this country were like their fruits and their flowers. The oranges might fall from the trees, but the blossoms would still be there. Husband and wives or lovers might die, but in the tropical hearts of these people it was not necessary that new affections should be formed, for they were already there, and needed only some one to receive them.

As he did not undertake his present expedition for the purpose of marrying ladies, no matter how beautiful they might be, it is quite natural that de Lussan should not accept the proffered hand of the young widow. But when she came to detail her plans, he found that it would be well worth his while to carefully consider her project.

The lady was by no means a thoughtless young creature, carried away by a sudden attachment. Before making known to de Lussan her preference for him above all other men, she had given the subject her most careful and earnest consideration, and had made plans which in her opinion would enable the buccaneer captain and herself to settle the matter to the satisfaction of all parties.

When de Lussan heard the lady's scheme, he was as much surprised by her businesslike ability as he had been by the declaration of her affection for him. She knew very well that he could not marry her and take her with him. Moreover, she did not wish to go. She had no fancy for such wild expeditions and such savage companions. Her plans were for peace and comfort and a happy domestic life. In a word, she desired that the handsome de Lussan should remain with her.

Of course the gentleman opened his eyes very wide when he heard this, but she had a great deal to say upon the subject, and she had not omitted any of the details which would be necessary for the success of her scheme.

The lady knew just as well as the buccaneer captain knew that the men under his command would not allow him to remain comfortably in that town with his share of the plunder, while they went on without a leader to undergo all sorts of hardships and dangers, perhaps defeat and death. If he announced his intention of withdrawing from the band, his enraged companions would probably kill him. Consequently a friendly separation between himself and his buccaneer followers was a thing not to be thought of, and she did not even propose it.

Her idea was a very different one. Just as soon as possible, that very night, de Lussan was to slip quietly out of the town, and make his way into the surrounding country. She would furnish him with a horse, and tell him the way he should take, and he was not to stop until he had reached a secluded spot, where she was quite sure the buccaneers would not be able to find him, no matter how diligently they might search. When they had entirely failed in every effort to discover their lost captain, who they would probably suppose had been killed by wandering Indians, — for it was impossible that he could have been murdered in the town without their knowledge, — they would give him up as lost and press on in search of further adventures.

When the buccaneers were far away, and all
danger from their return had entirely passed, then
the brave and polite Frenchman, now no longer a
buccaneer, could safely return to the town, where
the young widow would be most happy to marry
him, to lodge him in her handsome house, and to
make over to him all the large fortune and estates
which had been the property of her late husband.

This was a very attractive offer surely, a beautiful
woman, and a handsome fortune. But she offered
more than this. She knew that a gentleman who
had once captured and despoiled the town might
feel a little delicacy in regard to marrying and settling there and becoming one of its citizens, and
therefore she was prepared to remove any objections
which might be occasioned by such considerate
sentiments on his part.

She assured him that if he would agree to her
plan, she would use her influence with the authorities, and would obtain for him the position of city
treasurer, which her husband had formerly held.
And when he declared that such an astounding performance must be utterly impossible, she started
out immediately, and having interviewed the Governor of the town and other municipal officers,
secured their signature to a paper in which they
promised that if M. de Lussan would accept the
proposals which the lady had made, he would be

received most kindly by the officers and citizens of the town; that the position of treasurer would be given to him, and that all the promises of the lady should be made good.

Now our high-minded pirate was thrown into a great quandary, and although at first he had had no notion whatever of accepting the pleasant proposition which had been made to him by the young widow, he began to see that there were many good reasons why the affection, the high position, and the unusual advantages which she had offered to him might perhaps be the very best fortune which he could expect in this world.   In the first place, if he should marry this charming young creature and settle down as a respected citizen and an officer of the town, he would be entirely freed from the necessity of leading the life of a buccaneer, and this life was becoming more and more repugnant to him every day, — not only on account of the highly disagreeable nature of his associates and their reckless deeds, but because the country was becoming aroused, and the resistance to his advances was growing stronger and stronger.   In the next attack he made upon a town or village he might receive a musket ball in his body, which would end his career and leave his debts in France unpaid.

More than that, he was disappointed, as has been said before, in regard to the financial successes he

had expected. At that time he saw no immediate
prospect of being able to go home with money
enough in his pocket to pay off his creditors, and
if he did not return to his native land under those
conditions, he did not wish to return there at all.
Under these circumstances it seemed to be wise and
prudent, that if he had no reason to expect to be
able to settle down honorably and peaceably in
France, to accept this opportunity to settle honorably, peaceably, and in every way satisfactorily in
America.

It is easy to imagine the pitching and the tossing
in the mind of our French buccaneer. The more
he thought of the attractions of the fair widow and
of the wealth and position which had been offered
him, the more he hated all thoughts of his piratical
crew, and of the dastardly and cruel character of the
work in which they were engaged. If he could have
trusted the officers and citizens of the town, there is
not much doubt that he would have married the
widow, but those officers and citizens were Spaniards, and he was a Frenchman. A week before the
inhabitants of the place had been prosperous, contented, and happy. Now they had been robbed,
insulted, and in many cases ruined, and he was commander of the body of desperadoes who had robbed
and ruined them. Was it likely that they would
forget the injuries which he had inflicted upon them

simply because he had married a wealthy lady of the town and had kindly consented to accept the office of city treasurer ?

It was much more probable that when his men had really left that part of the country the citizens would forget all their promises to him and remember only his conduct toward them, and that even if he remained alive long enough to marry the lady and take the position offered him, it would not be long before she was again a widow and the office vacant.

So de Lussan shut his eyes to the tempting prospects which were spread out before him, and preferring rather to be a live buccaneer than a dead city treasurer, he told the beautiful widow that he could not marry her and that he must go forth again into the hard, unsympathetic world to fight, to burn, to steal, and to be polite. Then, fearing that if he remained he might find his resolution weakened, he gathered together his men and his pillage, and sadly went away, leaving behind him a joyful town and a weeping widow.

If the affection of the young Spanish lady for the buccaneer chief was sufficient to make her take an interest in his subsequent career, she would probably have been proud of him, for the ladies of those days had a high opinion of brave men and successful warriors. De Lussan soon proved that he was not

only a good fighter, but that he was also an able
general, and his operations on the western coast of
South America were more like military campaigns
than ordinary expeditions of lawless buccaneers.

He attacked and captured the city of Panama,
always an attractive prize to the buccaneer forces,
and after that he marched down the western coast
of South America, conquering and sacking many
towns. As he now carried on his business in a
somewhat wholesale way, it could not fail to bring
him in a handsome profit, and in the course of
time he felt that he was able to retire from the
active practice of his profession and to return to
France.

But as he was going back into the circles of
respectability, he wished to do so as a respectable
man. He discarded his hat and plume, he threw
away his great cutlass and his heavy pistols, and
attired in the costume of a gentleman in society he
prepared himself to enter again upon his old life.
He made the acquaintance of some of the French
colonial officers in the West Indies, and obtaining
from them letters of introduction to the Treasurer-
General of France, he went home as a gentleman
who had acquired a fortune by successful enterprises
in the new world.

The pirate who not only possesses a sense of propriety and a sensitive mind, but is also gifted with

an ability to write a book in which he describes his own actions and adventures, is to be credited with unusual advantages, and as Raveneau de Lussan possessed these advantages, he has come down to posterity as a high-minded pirate.

# Chapter XXI

## Exit Buccaneer; Enter Pirate

THE buccaneers of the West Indies and South America had grown to be a most formidable body of reckless freebooters. From merely capturing Spanish ships, laden with the treasures taken from the natives of the new world, they had grown strong enough to attack Spanish towns and cities. But when they became soldiers and marched in little armies, the patience of the civilized world began to weaken: Panama, for instance, was an important Spanish city; England was at peace with Spain; therefore, when a military force composed mainly of Englishmen, and led by a British subject, captured and sacked the said Spanish city, England was placed in an awkward position; if she did not interfere with her buccaneers, she would have a quarrel to settle with Spain.

Therefore it was that a new Governor was sent to Jamaica with strict orders to use every power he possessed to put down the buccaneers and to break up their organization, and it was to this end that he set a thief to catch thieves and empowered the ex-pirate, Morgan, to execute his former comrades.

But methods of conciliation, as well as threats of punishment, were used to induce the buccaneers to give up their illegal calling, and liberal offers were made to them to settle in Jamaica and become law-abiding citizens. They were promised grants of land and assistance of various kinds in order to induce them to take up the legitimate callings of planters and traders.

But these offers were not at all tempting to the Brethren of the Coast; from pirates *rampart* to pirates *couchant* was too great a change, and some of them, who found it impossible to embark on piratical cruises, on account of the increasing diffi-culties of fitting out vessels, returned to their origi-nal avocations of cattle-butchering and beef-drying, and some, it is said, chose rather to live among the wild Indians and share their independent lives, than to bind themselves to any form of honest industry.

The French had also been very active in sup-pressing the operations of their buccaneers, and now the Brethren of the Coast, considered as an organization for preying upon the commerce and settlers of Spain, might be said to have ceased to exist. But it must not be supposed that because buccaneering had died out, that piracy was dead.

If we tear down a wasps' nest, we destroy the abode
of a fierce and pitiless community, but we scatter
the wasps, and it is likely that each one of them,
in the unrestricted and irresponsible career to which
he has been unwillingly forced, will prove a much
more angry and dangerous insect than he had ever
been before.

This is what happened to these buccaneers who
would not give up a piratical life; driven away from
Jamaica, from San Domingo, and even from Tortuga, they retained a resting-place only at New
Providence, an island in the Bahamas, and this they
did not maintain very long.   Then they spread
themselves all over the watery world.   They were
no longer buccaneers, they were no longer brothers
of any sort or kind, they no longer set out merely
to pillage and fight the Spaniards, but their attacks
were made upon people of every nation.   English
ships and French ships, once safe from them, were
a welcome prey to these new pirates, unrestrained
by any kind of loyalty, even by any kind of enmity.
They were more rapacious, they were more cruel,
they were more like fiends than they had ever been
before.   They were cowardly and they no longer
proceeded against towns which might be defended,
nor ran up alongside of a man-of-war to boldly
board her in the very teeth of her guns.   They
confined themselves to attacks upon peaceable mer-

chant vessels, often robbing them and then scuttling them, delighted with the spectacle of a ship, with all its crew, sinking hopelessly into the sea. The scene of piratical operations in America was now very much changed. The successors of the Brothers of the Coast, no longer united by any bonds of fellowship, but each pirate captain acting independently in his own wicked way, was coming up from the West Indies to afflict the seacoast of our country.

The old buccaneers knew all about our southern coast, for they were among the very first white men who ever set foot on the shores of North and South Carolina before that region had been settled by colonists, and when the only inhabitants were the wild Indians. These early buccaneers often used its bays and harbors as convenient ports of refuge, where they could anchor, divide spoils, take in fresh water, and stay as long as they pleased without fear of molestation. It was natural enough that when the Spanish-hating buccaneer merged into the independent pirate, who respected no flag, and preyed upon ships of every nation, he should feel very much at home on the Carolina coasts.

As the country was settled, and Charles Town, now Charleston, grew to be a port of considerable importance, the pirates felt as much at home in this region as when it was inhabited merely by Indians.

They frequently touched at little seaside settlements, and boldly sailed into the harbor of Charles Town. But, unlike the unfortunate citizens of Porto Bello or Maracaibo, the American colonists were not frightened when they saw a pirate ship anchored in their harbors, for they knew its crew did not come as enemies, but as friendly traders.

The early English colonists were not as prosperous as they might have been if the mother country had not been so anxious to make money out of them. They were not allowed to import goods from any country but England, and if they had products or crops to export, they must be sold to English merchants. For whatever they bought they had to pay the highest prices, and they could not send into the markets of the world to get the best value for their own productions.

Therefore it was that a pirate ship was a very welcome visitor in Charles Town harbor. She was generally loaded with goods, which, as they were stolen, her captain could afford to sell very cheaply indeed, and as there was always plenty of Spanish gold on board, her crew was not apt to haggle very much in regard to the price of the spirits, the groceries, or the provisions which they bought from the merchants of the town. This friendly commerce between the pirates and the Carolinians grew to be so extensive that at one time the larger part of the

coin in circulation in those colonies consisted of
Spanish gold pieces, which had been brought
in and used by the pirates for the purchase of
goods.

But a pirate is very seldom a person of discretion,
who knows when to leave well enough alone, and
so, instead of contenting themselves with robbing
and capturing the vessels belonging to people whom
their Charles Town friends and customers would
look upon as foreigners, they boldly sailed up and
down the coast, seeking for floating booty wherever
they might find it, and when a pirate vessel commanded by an English captain and manned principally by an English crew, fell in with a big
merchantman flying the English flag, they bore
down upon that vessel, just as if it had been French,
or Spanish, or Dutch, and if the crew were impertinent enough to offer any resistance, they were cut
down and thrown overboard.

At last the pirates became so swaggeringly bold
and their captains so enterprising in their illegal
trading that the English government took vigorous measures, not only to break up piracy, but to
punish all colonists who should encourage the freebooters by commercial dealings with them. At
these laws the pirates laughed, and the colonists
winced, and there were many people in Charles
Town who vowed that if the King wanted them to

help him put down piracy, he must show them some
other way of getting imported goods at reasonable
prices.   So the pirates went on capturing merchantmen whenever they had a chance, and the Carolinians continued to look forward with interest to the
bargain days which always followed the arrival of a
pirate ship.   But this state of things did not last,
and the time came when the people of Charles
Town experienced a change of mind.   The planters
were now growing large quantities of rice, and
this crop became so valuable that the prosperity
of the colonies greatly increased.   And now the
pirates also became very much interested in the
rice crops, and when they had captured four or
five vessels sailing out of Charles Town heavily
laden with rice, the people of that town suddenly
became aware of the true character of a pirate.   He
was now in their eyes an unmitigated scoundrel who
not only stole goods from all nations, which he
brought to them and sold at low prices, but he actually stole their goods, their precious rice which they
were sending to England.

The indignant citizens of Charles Town took a
bold stand, and such a bold one it was that when
part of a crew of pirates, who had been put ashore
by their comrades on account of a quarrel, made
their way to the town, thinking they could tell a
tale of shipwreck and rely upon the friendship of

their old customers, they were taken into custody, and seven out of the nine were hanged.

The occasional repetition of such acts as this, and the exhibition of dangling pirates, hung up like scarecrows at the entrance of the harbors, dampened the ardor of the freebooters a good deal, and for some years they kept away from the harbor of Charles Town, which had once been to them such a friendly port.

# Chapter XXII

## The Great Blackbeard comes upon the Stage

SO long as the people of the Carolinas were prosperous and able to capture and execute pirates who interfered with their trade, the Atlantic sea-robbers kept away from their ports, but this prosperity did not last. Indian wars broke out, and in the course of time the colonies became very much weakened and impoverished, and then it was that the harbor of Charles Town began to be again interesting to the pirates.

About this time one of the most famous of sea-robbers was harassing the Atlantic coast of North America, and from New England to the West Indies, he was known as the great pirate Blackbeard. This man, whose real name was Thatch, was a most terrible fellow in appearance as well as action. He wore a long, heavy, black beard, which it was his fancy to separate into tails, each one tied with a colored ribbon, and often tucked behind his ears. Some of the writers of that day declared that the sight of this beard would create more terror in any

port of the American seaboard than would the
sudden appearance of a fiery comet. Across his
brawny breast he carried a sort of a sling in which
hung not less than three pairs of pistols in leathern
holsters, and these, in addition to his cutlass and a
knife or two in his belt, made him a most formidable-
looking fellow.

Some of the fanciful recreations of Blackbeard
show him to have been a person of consistent purpose. Even in his hours of rest when he was not
fighting or robbing, his savage soul demanded some
interesting excitement. Once he was seated at
table with his mate and two or three sailors, and
when the meal was over he took up a pair of
pistols, and cocking them put them under the table.
This peculiar action caused one of the sailors to
remember very suddenly that he had something to
do on deck, and he immediately disappeared. But
the others looked at their captain in astonishment,
wondering what he would do next. They soon
found out; for crossing the pistols, still under the
table, he fired them. One ball hit the mate in the
leg, but the other struck no one. When asked
what he meant by this strange action, he replied that
if he did not shoot one of his men now and then
they would forget what sort of a person he was.

At another time he invented a game ; he gathered
his officers and crew together and told them that

they were going to play that they were living in the
lower regions.  Thereupon the whole party followed
him down into the hold.  The hatches and all the
other openings were closed, and then Blackbeard
began to illuminate the scene with fire and brimstone.  The sulphur burned, the fumes rose, a
ghastly light spread over the countenances of the
desperadoes, and very soon some of them began to
gasp and cough and implore the captain to let in
some fresh air, but Blackbeard was bound to have
a good game, and he proceeded to burn more brimstone.  He laughed at the gasping fellows about
him and declared that he would be just as willing to
breathe the fumes of sulphur as common air.  When
at last he threw open the hatches, some of the men
were almost dead, but their stalwart captain had not
even sneezed.

In the early part of the eighteenth century Blackbeard made his headquarters in one of the inlets on
the North Carolina coast, and there he ruled as
absolute king, for the settlers in the vicinity seemed
to be as anxious to oblige him as the captains of the
merchantmen sailing along the coast were anxious
to keep out of his way.  On one of his voyages
Blackbeard went down the coast as far as Honduras,
where he took a good many prizes, and as some of
the crews of the captured vessels enlisted under him
he sailed north with a stronger force than ever

before, having a large ship of forty guns, three smaller vessels, and four hundred men. With this little fleet Blackbeard made for the coast of South Carolina, and anchored outside the harbor of Charles Town. He well understood the present condition of the place and was not in the least afraid that the citizens would hang him up on the shores of the bay.

Blackbeard began work without delay. Several well-laden ships — the Carolinians having no idea that pirates were waiting for them — came sailing out to sea and were immediately captured. One of these was a very important vessel, for it not only carried a valuable cargo, but a number of passengers, many of them people of note, who were on their way to England. One of these was a Mr. Wragg, who was a member of the Council of the Province. It might have been supposed that when Blackbeard took possession of this ship, he would have been satisfied with the cargo and the money which he found on board, and having no use for prominent citizens, would have let them go their way; but he was a trader as well as a plunderer, and he therefore determined that the best thing to do in this case was to put an assorted lot of highly respectable passengers upon the market and see what he could get for them. He was not at the time in need of money or provisions, but his men were very much

in want of medicines, so he decided to trade off his
prisoners for pills, potions, plasters, and all sorts of
apothecary's supplies.

He put three of his pirates in a boat, and with
them one of the passengers, a Mr. Marks, who was
commissioned as Blackbeard's special agent, with
orders to inform the Governor that if he did not
immediately send the medicines required, amount-
ing in value to about three hundred pounds, and
if he did not allow the pirate crew of the boat to
return in safety, every one of the prisoners would
be hanged from the yard-arm of his ship.

The boat rowed away to the distant town, and
Blackbeard waited two days for its return, and then
he grew very angry, for he believed that his messengers had been taken into custody, and he came
very near hanging Mr. Wragg and all his companions.  But before he began to satisfy his vengeance,
news came from the boat.  It had been upset in
the bay, and had had great trouble in getting to
Charles Town, but it had arrived there at last.
Blackbeard now waited a day or two longer; but
as no news came from Mr. Marks, he vowed he
would not be trifled with by the impudent people of Charles Town, and swore that every man,
woman, and child among the prisoners should
immediately prepare to be hanged.

Of course the unfortunate prisoners in the pirate

ship were in a terrible state of mind during the absence of Mr. Marks. They knew very well that they could expect no mercy from Blackbeard if the errand should be unsuccessful, and they also knew that the Charles Town people would not be likely to submit to such an outrageous demand upon them; so they trembled and quaked by day and by night, and when at last they were told to get ready to be hanged, every particle of courage left them, and they proposed to Blackbeard that if he would spare their lives, and that if it should turn out that their fellow-citizens had decided to sacrifice them for the sake of a few paltry drugs, they would take up the cause of the pirates; they would show Blackbeard the best way to sail into the harbor, and they would join with him and his men in attacking the city and punishing the inhabitants for their hard-hearted treatment of their unfortunate fellow-citizens.

This proposition pleased Blackbeard immensely; it would have been like a new game to take Mr. Wragg to the town and make him fight his fellow-members of the Council of the Province, and so he rescinded his order for a general execution, and bade his prisoners prepare to join with his pirates when he should give the word for an assault upon their city.

In the meantime there was a terrible stir in Charles Town. When the Governor and citizens

received the insolent and brutal message of Blackbeard they were filled with rage as well as consternation, and if there had been any way of going out
to sea to rescue their unhappy fellow-citizens, every
able-bodied man in the town would have enlisted in
the expedition.    But they had no vessels of war, and
they were not even in a position to arm any of the
merchantmen in the harbor.    It seemed to the
Governor and his council that there was nothing
for them to do but to submit to the demands of
Blackbeard, for they very well knew that he was a
scoundrel who would keep his word, and also that
whatever they did must be done quickly, for there
were the three swaggering pirates in the town, strutting about the streets as if they owned the place.
If this continued much longer, it would be impossible to keep the infuriated citizens from falling
upon these blustering rascals and bringing their impertinence to a summary end.    If this should happen, it would be a terrible thing, for not only would
Mr. Wragg and his companions be put to death,
but the pirates would undoubtedly attack the town,
which was in a very poor position for defence.

Consequently the drugs were collected with all
possible haste, and Mr. Marks and the pirates were
sent with them to Blackbeard.    We do not know
whether or not that bedizened cutthroat was satisfied with the way things turned out; for having

had the idea of going to Charles Town and obliging the prisoners to help him confiscate the drugs and chemicals, he may have preferred this unusual proceeding to a more commonplace transaction; but as the medicine had arrived he accepted it, and having secured all possible booty and money from the ships he had captured, and had stripped his prisoners of the greater part of their clothing, he set them on shore to walk to Charles Town as well as they could. They had a miserably difficult time, making their way through the woods and marshes, for there were women and children among them who were scarcely equal to the journey. One of the children was a little boy, the son of Mr. Wragg, who afterward became a very prominent man in the colonies. He rose to such a high position, not only among his countrymen, but in the opinion of the English government, that when he died, about the beginning of the Revolution, a tablet to his memory was placed in Westminster Abbey, which is, perhaps, the first instance of such an honor being paid to an American.

Having now provided himself with medicines enough to keep his wild crew in good physical condition, no matter how much they might feast and frolic on the booty they had obtained from Charles Town, Blackbeard sailed back to his North Carolina haunts and took a long vacation, during which time he managed to put himself on very good terms with the Governor and officials of the country. He had plenty of money and was willing to spend it, and so he was allowed to do pretty much as he pleased, provided he kept his purse open and did not steal from his neighbors.

But Blackbeard became tired of playing the part of a make-believe respectable citizen, and having spent the greater part of his money, he wanted to make some more. Consequently he fitted out a small vessel, and declaring that he was going on a legitimate commercial cruise, he took out regular papers for a port in the West Indies and sailed away, as if he had been a mild-mannered New England mariner going to catch codfish. The officials of the town of Bath, from which he sailed, came down to the ship and shook hands with him and hoped he would have good success.

After a moderate absence he returned to Bath, bringing with him a large French merchant vessel, with no people on board, but loaded with a valuable cargo of sugar and other goods. This vessel he declared he had found deserted at sea, and he therefore claimed it as a legitimate prize. Knowing the character of this bloody pirate, and knowing how very improbable it was that the captain and all the crew of a valuable merchant vessel, with nothing whatever the matter with her, would go out into

their boats and row away, leaving their ship to become the property of any one who might happen
along, it may seem surprising that the officials of
Bath appeared to have no doubt of the truth of
Blackbeard's story, and allowed him freely to land
the cargo on the French ship and store it away as
his own property.

But people who consort with pirates cannot be
expected to have very lively consciences, and although there must have been persons in the town
with intelligence enough to understand the story of
pitiless murder told by that empty vessel, whose
very decks and masts must have been regarded as
silent witnesses that her captain and crew did not
leave her of their own free will, no one in the town
interfered with the thrifty Blackbeard or caused any
public suspicion to fall upon the propriety of his
actions.

## Chapter XXIII

### A True-Hearted Sailor draws his Sword

FEELING now quite sure that he could do what he pleased on shore as well as at sea, Blackbeard swore more, swaggered more, and whenever he felt like it, sailed up and down the coast and took a prize or two to keep the pot boiling for himself and his men.

On one of these expeditions he went to Philadelphia, and having landed, he walked about to see what sort of a place it was, but the Governor of the state, hearing of his arrival, quickly arranged to let him know that the Quaker city allowed no black-hearted pirate, with a ribbon-bedecked beard, to promenade on Chestnut and Market streets, and promptly issued a warrant for the sea-robber's arrest. But Blackbeard was too sharp and too old a criminal to be caught in that way, and he left the city with great despatch.

The people along the coast of North Carolina became very tired of Blackbeard and his men. All sorts of depredations were committed on vessels, large and small, and whenever a ship was boarded and robbed or whenever a fishing-vessel was laid under contribution, Blackbeard was known to be at the bottom of the business, whether he personally appeared or not.   To have this busy pirate for a neighbor was extremely unpleasant, and the North Carolina settlers greatly longed to get rid of him. It was of no use for them to ask their own State Government to suppress this outrageous scoundrel, and although their good neighbor, South Carolina, might have been willing to help them, she was too poor at that time and had enough to do to take care of herself.

Not knowing, or not caring for the strong feeling of the settlers against him, Blackbeard continued in his wicked ways, and among other crimes he captured a small vessel and treated the crew in such a cruel and atrocious manner that the better class of North Carolinians vowed they would stand him no longer, and they therefore applied to Governor Spotswood, of Virginia, and asked his aid in putting down the pirates.   The Virginians were very willing to do what they could for their unfortunate neighbors.   The legislature offered a reward for the capture of Blackbeard or any of his men; but the Governor, feeling that this was not enough, determined to do something on his own responsibility,

for he knew very well that the time might come
when the pirate vessels would begin to haunt Virginia waters.

There happened to be at that time two small
British men-of-war in Hampton Roads, and although the Governor had no authority to send
these after the pirates, he fitted out two sloops at
his own expense and manned them with the best
fighting men from the war-vessels. One of the
sloops he put under Captain Brand, and the other
under Captain Maynard, both brave and experienced naval officers. All preparations were made
with the greatest secrecy — for if Blackbeard had
heard of what was going on, he would probably
have decamped — and then the two sloops went out
to sea with a commission from the Governor to capture Blackbeard, dead or alive. This was a pretty
heavy contract, but Brand and Maynard were cour-
ageous men and did not hesitate to take it.

The Virginians had been informed that the pirate
captain and his men were on a vessel in Ocracoke
Inlet, and when they arrived they found, to their
delight, that Blackbeard was there. When the
pirates saw the two armed vessels sailing into the
inlet, they knew very well that they were about to be
attacked, and it did not take them long to get ready
for a fight, nor did they wait to see what their enemy
was about to do. As soon as the sloops were near

enough, Blackbeard, without waiting for any prelimi-
nary exercises, such as a demand for surrender or
any nonsense of that sort, let drive at the intruders
with eight heavily loaded cannon.

Now the curtain had been rung up, and the play
began, and a very lively play it was. The guns
of the Virginians blazed away at the pirate ship,
and they would have sent out boats to board her
had not Blackbeard forestalled them. Boarding
was always a favorite method of fighting with the
pirates. They did not often carry heavy cannon,
and even when they did, they had but little fancy
for battles at long distances. What they liked was
to meet foes face to face and cut them down on
their own decks. In such combats they felt at
home, and were almost always successful, for there
were few mariners or sailors, even in the British
navy, who could stand against these brawny, glar-
ing-eyed dare-devils, who sprang over the sides of
a vessel like panthers, and fought like bulldogs.
Blackbeard had had enough cannonading, and he
did not wait to be boarded. Springing into a
boat with about twenty of his men, he rowed to
the vessel commanded by Maynard, and in a
few minutes he and his pirates surged on board
her.

Now there followed on the decks of that sloop
one of the most fearful hand-to-hand combats

known to naval history.　Pirates had often attacked
vessels where they met with strong resistance, but
never had a gang of sea-robbers fallen in with such
bold and skilled antagonists as those who now confronted Blackbeard and his crew.　At it they went,
— cut, fire, slash, bang, howl, and shout.　Steel
clashed, pistols blazed, smoke went up, and blood
ran down, and it was hard in the confusion for a
man to tell friend from foe.　Blackbeard was everywhere, bounding from side to side, as he swung his
cutlass high and low, and though many a shot was
fired at him, and many a rush made in his direction,
every now and then a sailor went down beneath his
whirling blade.

But the great pirate had not boarded that ship
to fight with common men.　He was looking for
Maynard, the commander.　Soon he met him, and
for the first time in his life he found his match.
Maynard was a practised swordsman, and no matter how hard and how swiftly came down the cutlass
of the pirate, his strokes were always evaded, and
the sword of the Virginian played more dangerously
near him.　At last Blackbeard, finding that he could
not cut down his enemy, suddenly drew a pistol,
and was about to empty its barrels into the very
face of his opponent, when Maynard sent his sword-
blade into the throat of the furious pirate; the
great Blackbeard went down upon his back on the

"Maynard was a practised swordsman, and the great Blackbeard
went down upon his back." — p. 214.

deck, and in the next moment Maynard put an end to his nefarious career. Their leader dead, the few pirates who were left alive gave up the fight, and sprang overboard, hoping to be able to swim ashore, and the victory of the Virginians was complete.

The strength, toughness, and extraordinary vitality of these feline human beings, who were known as pirates, has often occasioned astonishment in ordinary people. Their sun-tanned and hairy bodies seemed to be made of something like wire, leather, and India rubber, upon which the most tremendous exertions, and even the infliction of severe wounds, made but little impression. Before Blackbeard fell, he received from Maynard and others no less than twenty-five wounds, and yet he fought fearlessly to the last, and when the panting officer sheathed his sword, he felt that he had performed a most signal deed of valor.

When they had broken up the pirate nest in Ocracoke Inlet, the two sloops sailed to Bath, where they compelled some of the unscrupulous town officials to surrender the cargo which had been stolen from the French vessel and stored in the town by Blackbeard; then they sailed proudly back to Hampton Roads, with the head of the dreaded Blackbeard dangling from the end of the bowsprit of the vessel he had boarded, and on whose deck he had discovered the fact, before unknown to him, that a well-trained, honest man can fight as well as the most reckless cutthroat who ever decked his beard with ribbons, and swore enmity to all things good.

# Chapter XXIV

## A Greenhorn under the Black Flag

EARLY in the eighteenth century there lived at Bridgetown, in the island of Barbadoes, a very pleasant, middle-aged gentleman named Major Stede Bonnet. He was a man in comfortable circumstances, and had been an officer in the British army. He had retired from military service, and had bought an estate at Bridgetown, where he lived in comfort and was respected by his neighbors.

But for some reason or other this quiet and reputable gentleman got it into his head that he would like to be a pirate. There were some persons who said that this strange fancy was due to the fact that his wife did not make his home pleasant for him, but it is quite certain that if a man wants an excuse for robbing and murdering his fellow-beings he ought to have a much better one than the bad temper of his wife. But besides the general reasons why Major Bonnet should not become a pirate, and which applied to all men as well as himself, there was a special reason against his adoption of the profession of a sea-robber, for he was an out-and-out landsman and knew nothing whatever of nautical matters. He had been at sea but very little, and if he had heard a boatswain order his man to furl the keel, to batten down the shrouds, or to hoist the forechains to the topmast yard, he would have seen nothing out of the way in these commands. He was very fond of history, and very well read in the literature of the day. He was accustomed to the habits of good society, and knew a great deal about farming and horses, cows and poultry, but if he had been compelled to steer a vessel, he would not have known how to keep her bow ahead of her stern.

But notwithstanding this absolute incapacity for such a life, and the absence of any of the ordinary motives for abandoning respectability and entering upon a career of crime, Major Bonnet was determined to become a pirate, and he became one. He had money enough to buy a ship and to fit her out and man her, and this he quietly did at Bridgetown, nobody supposing that he was going to do anything more than start off on some commercial cruise. When everything was ready, his vessel slipped out of the harbor one night, and after he was sailing safely on the rolling sea he stood upon the quarter-deck and proclaimed himself a pirate. It might not be supposed that this was necessary, for the seventy men on board his ship were all desperate cutthroats, of various nationalities, whom he had found in the little port, and who knew very well what was expected of them when they reached the sea.   But if Stede Bonnet had not proclaimed himself a pirate, it is possible that he might not have believed, himself, that he was one, and so he ran up the black flag, with its skeleton or skull and cross-bones, he girded on a great cutlass, and, folding his arms, he ordered his mate to steer the vessel to the coast of Virginia.

Although Bonnet knew so little about ships and the sea, and had had no experience in piracy, his men were practised seamen, and those of them who had not been pirates before were quite ready and very well fitted to become such ; so when this green hand came into the waters of Virginia he actually took two or three vessels and robbed them of their cargoes, burning the ships, and sending the crews on shore.

This had grown to be a common custom among the pirates, who, though cruel and hard-hearted, had not the inducements of the old buccaneers to torture and murder the crews of the vessels which they captured.   They could not hate human beings in general as the buccaneers hated the Spaniards, and so they were a little more humane to their prisoners, setting them ashore on some island or desert coast, and letting them shift for themselves as best they might. This was called marooning, and was some-what less heartless than the old methods of getting rid of undesirable prisoners by drowning or behead-ing them.

As Bonnet had always been rather conventional in his ideas and had respected the customs of the society in which he found himself, he now adopted all the piratical fashions of the day, and when he found himself too far from land to put the captured crew on shore, he did not hesitate to make them " walk the plank," which was a favorite device of the pirates whenever they had no other way of disposing of their prisoners. The unfortunate wretches, with their hands tied behind them, were compelled, one by one, to mount a plank which was projected over the side of the vessel and balanced like a see-saw, and when, prodded by knives and cutlasses, they stepped out upon this plank, of course it tipped up, and down they went into the sea. In this way, men, women, and children slipped out of sight among the waves as the vessel sailed merrily on.

In one branch of his new profession Bonnet rap-idly became proficient. He was an insatiable robber and a cruel conqueror. He captured merchant vessels all along the coast as high up as New Eng-land, and then he came down again and stopped for a while before Charles Town harbor, where he took a couple of prizes, and then put into one of the North Carolina harbors, where it was always easy for a pirate vessel to refit and get ready for further adventures.

Bonnet's vessel was named the *Revenge*, which was about as ill suited to the vessel as her commander was ill fitted to sail her, for Bonnet had nobody to revenge himself upon unless, indeed, it were his scolding wife. But a good many pirate ships were then called the *Revenge*, and Bonnet was bound to follow the fashion, whatever it might be.

Very soon after he had stood upon the quarter-deck and proclaimed himself a pirate his men had discovered that he knew no more about sailing than he knew about painting portraits, and although there were under-officers who directed all the nautical operations, the mass of the crew conceived a great contempt for a landsman captain. There was much grumbling and growling, and many of the men would have been glad to throw Bonnet overboard and take the ship into their own hands. But when any symptoms of mutiny showed themselves, the pirates found that although they did not have a sailor in command over them, they had a very determined and relentless master. Bonnet knew that the captain of a pirate ship ought to be the most severe and rigid man on board, and so, at the slightest sign of insubordination, his grumbling men were put in chains

or flogged, and it was Bonnet's habit at such times
to strut about the deck with loaded pistols, threatening to blow out the brains of any man who dared to
disobey him.    Recognizing that although their captain was no sailor he was a first-class tyrant, the
rebellious crew kept their grumbling to themselves
and worked his ship.

Bonnet now pointed the bow of the *Revenge*
southward — that is, he requested somebody else to
see that it was done — and sailed to the Bay of
Honduras, which was a favorite resort of the pirates
about that time.    And here it was that he first met
with the famous Captain Blackbeard.    There can be
no doubt that our amateur pirate was very glad indeed
to become acquainted with this well-known professional, and they soon became good friends.    Blackbeard was on the point of organizing an expedition,
and he proposed that Bonnet and his vessel should
join it.    This invitation was gladly accepted, and
the two pirate captains started out on a cruise together.    Now the old reprobate, Blackbeard, knew
everything about ships and was a good navigator,
and it was not long before he discovered that his
new partner was as green as grass in regard to all
nautical affairs.    Consequently, after having thought
the matter over for a time, he made up his mind
that Bonnet was not at all fit to command such a
fine vessel as the one he owned and had fitted out,

" Blackbeard told Bonnet that he was not fit to be a pirate captain, and that he would send somebody to take charge of the *Revenge*." — p. 223.

and as pirates make their own laws, and perhaps do not obey them if they happen not to feel like it, Blackbeard sent for Bonnet to come on board his ship, and then, in a manner as cold-blooded as if he had been about to cut down a helpless prisoner, Blackbeard told Bonnet that he was not fit to be a pirate captain, that he intended to keep him on board his own vessel, and that he would send somebody to take charge of the *Revenge*.

This was a fall indeed, and Bonnet was almost stunned by it.   An hour before he had been proudly strutting about on the deck of a vessel which belonged to him, and in which he had captured many valuable prizes, and now he was told he was to stay on Blackbeard's ship and make himself useful in keeping the log book, or in doing any other easy thing which he might happen to understand.   The green pirate ground his teeth and swore bitterly inside of himself, but he said nothing openly; on Blackbeard's ship Blackbeard's decisions were not to be questioned.

# Chapter XXV

## Bonnet again to the Front

IT must not be supposed that the late commander of the *Revenge* continued to be satisfied, as he sat in the cabin of Blackbeard's vessel and made the entries of the day's sailing and various performances. He obeyed the orders of his usurping partner because he was obliged to do so, but he did not hate Blackbeard any the less because he had to keep quiet about it. He accompanied his pirate chief on various cruises, among which was the famous expedition to the harbor of Charles Town where Blackbeard traded Mr. Wragg and his companions for medicines.

Having a very fine fleet under him, Blackbeard did a very successful business for some time, but feeling that he had earned enough for the present, and that it was time for him to take one of his vacations, he put into an inlet in North Carolina, where he disbanded his crew. So long as he was on shore spending his money and having a good time, he did not want to have a lot of men about him who would look to him to support them when they had spent their portion of the spoils.    Having no further use for Bonnet, he dismissed him also, and did not object to his resuming possession of his own vessel.    If the green pirate chose to go to sea again and perhaps drown himself and his crew, it was a matter of no concern to Blackbeard.

But this was a matter of very great concern to Stede Bonnet, and he proceeded to prove that there were certain branches of the piratical business in which he was an adept, and second to none of his fellow-practitioners.    He wished to go pirating again, and saw a way of doing this which he thought would be far superior to any of the common methods.    It was about this time that King George of England, very desirous of breaking up piracy, issued a proclamation in which he promised pardon to any pirate who would appear before the proper authorities, renounce his evil practices, and take an oath of allegiance.    It also happened that very soon after this proclamation had been issued, England went to war with Spain.    Being a man who kept himself posted in the news of the world, so far as it was possible, Bonnet saw in the present state of affairs a very good chance for him to play the part of a wolf in sheep's clothing, and he proceeded to begin his new piratical career by renouncing piracy.    So leaving the *Revenge* in the inlet, he journeyed overland to

Bath; there he signed pledges, took oaths, and did
everything that was necessary to change himself
from a pirate captain to a respectable commander
of a duly authorized British privateer. Returning
to his vessel with all the papers in his pocket necessary to prove that he was a loyal and law-abiding
subject of Great Britain, he took out regular clear-
ance papers for St. Thomas, which was a British
naval station, and where he declared he was going
in order to obtain a commission as a privateer.

Now the wily Bonnet had everything he wanted
except a crew. Of course it would not do for him,
in his present respectable capacity, to go about en-
listing unemployed pirates, but at this point fortune
again favored him; he knew of a desert island not
very far away where Blackbeard, at the end of his
last cruise, had marooned a large party of his men.
This heartless pirate had not wanted to take all of
his followers into port, because they might prove
troublesome and expensive to him, and so he had
put a number of them on this island, to live or die
as the case might be. Bonnet went over to this
island, and finding the greater part of these men still
surviving, he offered to take them to St. Thomas
in his vessel if they would agree to work the ship
to port. This proposition was of course joyfully
accepted, and very soon the *Revenge* was manned
with a complete crew of competent desperadoes.

All these operations took a good deal of time, and, at last, when everything was ready for Bonnet to start out on his piratical cruise, he received information which caused him to change his mind, and to set forth on an errand of a very different kind. He had supposed that Blackbeard, whom he had never forgiven for the shameful and treacherous manner in which he had treated him, was still on shore enjoying himself, but he was told by the captain of a small trading vessel that the old pirate was preparing for another cruise, and that he was then in Ocracoke Inlet. Now Bonnet folded his arms and stamped his feet upon the quarter-deck. The time had come for him to show that the name of his vessel meant something. Never before had he had an opportunity for revenging himself on anybody, but now that hour had arrived. He would revenge himself upon Blackbeard!

The implacable Bonnet sailed out to sea in a truly warlike frame of mind. He was not going forth to prey upon unresisting merchantmen; he was on his way to punish a black-hearted pirate, a faithless scoundrel, who had not only acted knavishly toward the world in general, but had behaved most disloyally and disrespectfully toward a fellow pirate chief. If he could once run the *Revenge* alongside the ship of the perfidious Blackbeard, he would show him what a green hand could do.

When Bonnet reached Ocracoke Inlet, he was deeply disappointed to find that Blackbeard had left that harbor, but he did not give up the pursuit. He made hot chase after the vessel of his pirate enemy, keeping a sharp lookout in hopes of discovering some signs of him. If the enraged Bonnet could have met the ferocious Blackbeard face to face, there might have been a combat which would have relieved the world of two atrocious villains, and Captain Maynard would have been deprived of the honor of having slain the most famous pirate of the day.

Bonnet was a good soldier and a brave man, and although he could not sail a ship, he understood the use of the sword even better, perhaps, than Blackbeard, and there is good reason to believe that if the two ships had come together, their respective crews would have allowed their captains to fight out their private quarrel without interference, for pirates delight in a bloody spectacle, and this would have been to them a rare diversion of the kind.

But Bonnet never overtook Blackbeard, and the great combat between the rival pirates did not take place. After vainly searching for a considerable time for a trace or sight of Blackbeard, the baffled Bonnet gave up the pursuit and turned his mind to other objects. The first thing he did was to change

the name of his vessel; if he could not be revenged, he would not sail in the *Revenge*. Casting
about in his mind for a good name, he decided to
call her the *Royal James*. Having no intention of
respecting his oaths or of keeping his promises, he
thought that, as he was going to be disloyal, he
might as well be as disloyal as he could, and so he
gave his ship the name assumed by the son of James
the Second, who was a pretender to the throne, and
was then in France plotting against the English government.

The next thing he did was to change his own
name, for he thought this would make matters better for him if he should be captured after entering
upon his new criminal career. So he called himself
Captain Thomas, by which name he was afterwards
known.

When these preliminaries had been arranged, he
gathered his crew together and announced that instead of going to St. Thomas to get a commission
as a privateer, he had determined to keep on in his
old manner of life, and that he wished them to
understand that not only was he a pirate captain,
but that they were a pirate crew. Many of the men
were very much surprised at this announcement,
for they had thought it a very natural thing for
the green-hand Bonnet to give up pirating after he
had been so thoroughly snubbed by Blackbeard, and

they had not supposed that he would ever think
again of sailing under a black flag.

However, the crew's opinion of the green-hand
captain had been a good deal changed. In his various
cruises he had learned a good deal about navigation,
and could now give very fair orders, and his furious
pursuit of Blackbeard had also given him a reputation for reckless bravery which he had not enjoyed
before. A man who was chafing and fuming for a
chance of a hand-to-hand conflict with the greatest
pirate of the day must be a pretty good sort of
a fellow from their point of view. Moreover, their
strutting and stalking captain, so recently balked of
his dark revenge, was a very savage-looking man,
and it would not be pleasant either to try to persuade
him to give up his piratical intention, or to decline
to join him in carrying it out; so the whole of the
crew, minor officers and men, changed their minds
about going to St. Thomas, and agreed to hoist
the skull and cross-bones, and to follow Captain
Bonnet wherever he might lead.

Bonnet now cruised about in grand style and
took some prizes on the Virginia coast, and then
went up into Delaware Bay, where he captured such
ships as he wanted, and acted generally in the most
domineering and insolent fashion. Once, when he
stopped near the town of Lewes, in order to send
some prisoners ashore, he sent a message to the offi-

cers of the town to the effect that if they interfered
with his men when they came ashore, he would open
fire upon the town with his cannon, and blow every
house into splinters.  Of course the citizens, having
no way of defending themselves, were obliged to
allow the pirates to come on shore and depart
unmolested.

Then after this the blustering captain captured
two valuable sloops, and wishing to take them along
with him without the trouble of transferring their
cargoes to his own vessel, he left their crews on
board, and ordered them to follow him wherever he
went.  Some days after that, when one of the
vessels seemed to be sailing at too great a distance,
Bonnet quickly let her captain know that he was
not a man to be trifled with, and sent him the message that if he did not keep close to the *Royal James*,
he would fire into him and sink him to the bottom.

After a time Bonnet put into a North Carolina
port in order to repair the *Royal James*, which was
becoming very leaky, and seeing no immediate
legitimate way of getting planks and beams enough
with which to make the necessary repairs, he captured a small sloop belonging in the neighborhood,
and broke it up in order to get the material he
needed to make his own vessel seaworthy.

Now the people of the North Carolina coast very
seldom interfered with pirates, as we have seen, and

it is likely that Bonnet might have stayed in port as long as he pleased, and repaired and refitted his vessel without molestation if he had bought and paid for the planks and timber he required. But when it came to boldly seizing their property, that was too much even for the people of the region, and complaints of Bonnet's behavior spread from settlement to settlement, and it very soon became known all down the coast that there was a pirate in North Carolina who was committing depredations there and was preparing to set out on a fresh cruise.

When these tidings came to Charles Town, the citizens were thrown into great agitation. It had not been long since Blackbeard had visited their harbor, and had treated them with such brutal insolence, and there were bold spirits in the town who declared that if any effort by them could prevent another visitation of the pirates, that effort should be made. There was no naval force in the harbor which could be sent out to meet the pirates, who were coming down the coast; but Mr. William Rhett, a private gentleman of position in the place, went to the Governor and offered to fit out, at his own expense, an expedition for the purpose of turning away from their city the danger which threatened it.

# Chapter XXVI

## The Battle of the Sand Bars

WHEN that estimable private gentleman, Mr. William Rhett, of Charles Town, had received a commission from the Governor to go forth on his own responsibility and meet the dreaded pirate, the news of whose depredations had thrown the good citizens into such a fever of apprehension, he took possession, in the name of the law, of two large sloops, the *Henry* and the *Sea-Nymph*, which were in the harbor, and at his own expense he manned them with well-armed crews, and put on board of each of them eight small cannon. When everything was ready, Mr. Rhett was in command of a very formidable force for those waters, and if he had been ready to sail a few days sooner, he would have had an opportunity of giving his men some practice in fighting pirates before they met the particular and more important sea-robber whom they had set out to encounter. Just as his vessel was ready to sail, Mr. Rhett received news that a pirate ship had captured two or three merchantmen just outside the harbor, and he put out to sea with all possible haste and cruised up and down the coast for some time, but he did not find this most recent depredator, who had departed very promptly when he heard that armed ships were coming out of the harbor.

Now Mr. Rhett, who was no more of a sailor than Stede Bonnet had been when he first began his seafaring life, boldly made his way up the coast to the mouth of Cape Fear River, where he had been told the pirate vessel was lying. When he reached his destination, Mr. Rhett found that it would not be an easy thing to ascend the river, for the reason that the pilots he had brought with him knew nothing about the waters of that part of the coast, and although the two ships made their way very cautiously, it was not long after they had entered the river before they got out of the channel, and it being low tide, both of them ran aground upon sand bars.

This was a very annoying accident, but it was not disastrous, for the sailing masters who commanded the sloops knew very well that when the tide rose, their vessels would float again. But it prevented Mr. Rhett from going on and making an immediate attack upon the pirate vessel, the topmasts of which could be plainly seen behind a high headland some distance up the river.

Of course Bonnet, or Captain Thomas, as he now

chose to be called, soon became aware of the fact that two good-sized vessels were lying aground near the mouth of the river, and having a very natural curiosity to see what sort of craft they were, he waited until nightfall and then sent three armed boats to make observations. When these boats returned to the *Royal James* and reported that the grounded vessels were not well-loaded trading craft, but large sloops full of men and armed with cannon, Bonnet (for we prefer to call him by his old name) had good reason to fold his arms, knit his brows, and strut up and down the deck. He was sure that the armed vessels came from Charles Town, and there was no reason to doubt that if the Governor of South Carolina had sent two ships against him the matter was a very serious one. He was penned up in the river, he had only one fighting vessel to contend against two, and if he could not succeed in getting out to sea before he should be attacked by the Charles Town ships, there would be but little chance of his continuing in his present line of business. If the *Royal James* had been ready to sail, there is no doubt that Bonnet would have taken his chance of finding the channel in the dark, and would have sailed away that night without regard to the cannonading which might have been directed against him from the two stranded vessels.

But as it was impossible to get ready to sail,

Bonnet went to work with the greatest energy to get ready to fight. He knew that when the tide rose there would be two armed sloops afloat, and that there would be a regular naval battle on the quiet waters of Cape Fear River. All night his men worked to clear the decks and get everything in order for the coming combat, and all night Mr. Rhett and his crews kept a sharp watch for any unexpected move of the enemy, while they loaded their guns, their pistols, and their cannon, and put everything in order for action.

Very early in the morning the wide-awake crews of the South Carolina vessels, which were now afloat and at anchor, saw that the topmasts of the pirate craft were beginning to move above the distant headland, and very soon Bonnet's ship came out into view, under full sail, and as she veered around they saw that she was coming toward them. Up went the anchors and up went the sails of the *Henry* and the *Sea-Nymph*, and the naval battle between the retired army officer who had almost learned to be a sailor, and the private gentleman from South Carolina, who knew nothing whatever about managing ships, was about to begin.

It was plain to the South Carolinians that the great object of the pirate captain was to get out to sea just as soon as he could, and that he was coming down the river, not because he wished to make an

immediate attack upon them, but because he hoped
to slip by them and get away. Of course they
could follow him upon the ocean and fight him if
their vessels were fast enough, but once out of the
river with plenty of sea-room, he would have twenty
chances of escape where now he had one.

But Mr. Rhett did not intend that the pirates
should play him this little trick; he wanted to fight
the dastardly wretches in the river, where they
could not get away, and he had no idea of letting
them sneak out to sea. Consequently as the *Royal
James*, under full sail, was making her way down
the river, keeping as far as possible from her two
enemies, Mr. Rhett ordered his ships to bear down
upon her so as to cut off her retreat and force her
toward the opposite shore of the river. This ma-
nœuvre was performed with great success. The two
Charles Town sloops sailed so boldly and swiftly
toward the *Royal James* that the latter was obliged
to hug the shore, and the first thing the pirates
knew they were stuck fast and tight upon a sand bar.
Three minutes afterward the *Henry* ran upon a
sand bar, and there being enough of these obstruc-
tions in that river to satisfy any ordinary demand,
the *Sea-Nymph* very soon grounded herself upon
another of them. But unfortunately she took up
her permanent position at a considerable distance
from her consort.

Here now were the vessels which were to conduct
this memorable sea-fight, all three fast in the sand
and unable to move, and their predicament was
made the worse by the fact that it would be five
hours before the tide would rise high enough for
any one of them to float. The positions of the
three vessels were very peculiar and awkward ; the
*Henry* and the *Royal James* were lying so near to
each other that Mr. Rhett could have shot Major
Bonnet with a pistol if the latter gentleman had
given him the chance, and the *Sea-Nymph* was so
far away that she was entirely out of the fight, and
her crew could do nothing but stand and watch
what was going on between the other two vessels.

But although they could not get any nearer each
other, nor get away from each other, the pirates and
Mr. Rhett's crew had no idea of postponing the
battle until they should be afloat and able to fight
in the ordinary fashion of ships; they immediately
began to fire at each other with pistols, muskets, and
cannon, and the din and roar was something that
must have astonished the birds and beasts and fishes
of that quiet region.

As the tide continued to run out of the river, and
its waters became more and more shallow, the two
contending vessels began to careen over to one side,
and, unfortunately for the *Henry*, they both careened
in the same direction, and in such a manner that the

deck of the *Royal James* was inclined away from the *Henry*, while the deck of the latter leaned toward her pirate foe. This gave a great advantage to Bonnet and his crew, for they were in a great measure protected by the hull of their vessel, whereas the whole deck of the *Henry* was exposed to the fire of the pirates. But Mr. Rhett and his South Carolinians were all brave men, and they blazed away with their muskets and pistols at the pirates whenever they could see a head above the rail of the *Royal James*, while with their cannon they kept firing at the pirate's hull.

For five long hours the fight continued, but the cannon carried by the two vessels must have been of very small calibre, for if they had been firing at such short range and for such a length of time with modern guns, they must have shattered each other into kindling wood. But neither vessel seems to have been seriously injured, and although there were a good many men killed on both sides, the combat was kept up with great determination and fury. At one time it seemed almost certain that Bonnet would get the better of Mr. Rhett, and he ordered his black flag waved contemptuously in the air while his men shouted to the South Carolinians to come over and call upon them, but the South Carolina boys answered these taunts with cheers and fired away more furiously than ever.

The tide was now coming in, and everybody on
board the two fighting vessels knew very well that
the first one of them which should float would have
a great advantage over the other, and would probably
be the conqueror.   In came the tide, and still the
cannons roared and the muskets cracked, while the
hearts of the pirates and the South Carolinians
almost stood still as they each watched the other
vessel to see if she showed any signs of floating.

At last such signs were seen ; the *Henry* was further from the shore than the *Royal James*, and she
first felt the influence of the rising waters.   Her
masts began to straighten, and at last her deck was
level, and she floated clear of the bottom while her
antagonist still lay careened over on her side.   Now
the pirates saw there was no chance for them ; in a
very short time the other Carolina sloop would be
afloat, and then the two vessels would bear down
upon them and utterly destroy both them and their
vessel.   Consequently upon the *Royal James* there
was a general disposition to surrender and to make
the best terms they could, for it would be a great
deal better to submit and run the chance of a trial
than to keep up the fight against enemies so much
superior both in numbers and ships, who would
soon be upon them.

But Bonnet would not listen to one word of
surrender.   Rather than give up the fight he de-

clared he would set fire to the powder magazine of the *Royal James* and blow himself, his ship, and his men high up into the air.  Although he had not a sailor's skill, he possessed a soldier's soul, and in spite of his being a dastardly and cruel pirate he was a brave man.  But Bonnet was only one, and his crew numbered dozens, and notwithstanding his furiously dissenting voice it was determined to surrender, and when Mr. Rhett sailed up to the *Royal James*, intending to board her if the pirates still showed resistance, he found them ready to submit to terms and to yield themselves his prisoners.

Thus ended the great sea-fight between the private gentlemen, and thus ended Stede Bonnet's career. He and his men were taken to Charles Town, where most of the pirate crew were tried and executed. The green-hand pirate, who had wrought more devastation along the American coast than many a skilled sea-robber, was held in custody to await his trial, and it seems very strange that there should have been a public sentiment in Charles Town which induced the officials to treat this pirate with a certain degree of respect simply from the fact that his station in life had been that of a gentleman.  He was a much more black-hearted scoundrel than any of his men, but they were executed as soon as possible while his trial was postponed and he was allowed privileges which would never have been accorded a common pirate. In consequence of this leniency he escaped and had to be retaken by Mr. Rhett. It was so long before he was tried that sympathy for his misfortunes arose among some of the tender-hearted citizens of Charles Town whose houses he would have pillaged and whose families he would have murdered if the exigencies of piracy had rendered such action desirable.

Finding that other people were trying to save his life, Bonnet came down from his high horse and tried to save it himself by writing piteous letters to the Governor, begging for mercy. But the Governor of South Carolina had no notion of sparing a pirate who had deliberately put himself under the protection of the law in order that he might better pursue his lawless and wicked career, and the green hand, with the black heart, was finally hung on the same spot where his companions had been executed.

# Chapter XXVII

## A Six Weeks' Pirate

ABOUT the time of Stede Bonnet's terminal adventures a very unpretentious pirate made his appearance in the waters of New York. This was a man named Richard Worley, who set himself up in piracy in a very small way, but who, by a strict attention to business, soon achieved a remarkable success. He started out as a scourge upon the commerce of the Atlantic Ocean with only an open boat and eight men. In this small craft he went down the coast of New Jersey taking everything he could from fishing boats and small trading vessels until he reached Delaware Bay, and here he made a bold stroke and captured a good-sized sloop.

When this piratical outrage was reported at Philadelphia, it created a great sensation, and people talked about it until the open boat with nine men grew into a great pirate ship filled with roaring desperadoes and cutthroats. From Philadelphia the news was sent to New York, and that government was

warned of the great danger which threatened the
coast.    As soon as this alarming intelligence was
received, the New Yorkers set to work to get up an
expedition which should go out to sea and endeavor
to destroy the pirate vessel before it could enter
their port, and work havoc among their merchantmen.

It may seem strange that a small open boat with
nine men could stir up such a commotion in these
two great provinces of North America, but if we can
try to imagine the effect which would be produced
among the inhabitants of Staten Island, or in the
hearts of the dwellers in the beautiful houses on the
shores of the Delaware River, by the announcement
that a boat carrying nine desperate burglars was to
be expected in their neighborhood, we can better
understand what the people of New York and
Philadelphia thought when they heard that Worley
had captured a sloop in Delaware Bay.

The expedition which left New York made a very
unsuccessful cruise.    It sailed for days and days,
but never saw a sign of a boat containing nine men,
and it returned disappointed and obliged to report
no progress.    With Worley, however, progress had
been very decided.    He captured another sloop, and
this being a large one and suitable to his purposes,
he took possession of it, gave up his open boat, and
fitted out his prize as a regular piratical craft.    With

a good ship under his command, Captain Worley now enlarged his sphere of action; on both shores of Delaware Bay, and along the coast of New Jersey, he captured everything which came in his way, and for about three weeks he made the waters in those regions very hot for every kind of peaceable commercial craft. If Worley had been in trade, his motto would have been "Quick sales and small profits," for by day and by night, the *New York's Revenge*, which was the name he gave to his new vessel, cruised east and west and north and south, losing no opportunity of levying contributions of money, merchandise, food, and drink upon any vessel, no matter how insignificant it might be.

The Philadelphians now began to tremble in their shoes; for if a boat had so quickly grown into a sloop, the sloop might grow into a fleet, and they had all heard of Porto Bello, and the deeds of the bloody buccaneers. The Governor of Pennsylvania, recognizing the impending danger and the necessity of prompt action, sent to Sandy Hook, where there was a British man-of-war, the *Phœnix*, and urged that this vessel should come down into Delaware Bay and put an end to the pirate ship which was ravaging those waters. Considering that Worley had not been engaged in piracy for much more than four weeks, he had created a reputation for enterprise and industry, which gave him a very important

position as a commerce destroyer, and a large man-
of-war did not think that he was too small game for
her to hunt down, and so she set forth to capture or
destroy the audacious Worley. But never a Worley
of any kind did she see. While the *Phœnix* was
sailing along the coast, examining all the coves and
harbors of New Jersey and Pennsylvania, the *New
York's Revenge* put out to sea, and then proceeded
southward to discover a more undisturbed field of
operation.

We will now leave Worley's vessel sailing
southward, and go for a time to Charles Town,
where some very important events were taking
place. The Governor of South Carolina had been
very much afraid that the pirates in general would
take some sort of revenge for the capture of Stede
Bonnet, who was then in prison awaiting trial, and
that if he should be executed, Charles Town might
be visited by an overpowering piratical force, and
he applied to England to have a war-vessel sent to
the harbor. But before any relief of this kind
could be expected, news came to Charles Town
that already a celebrated pirate, named Moody, was
outside of the harbor, capturing merchant vessels,
and it might be that he was only waiting for the
arrival of other pirate ships to sail into the harbor
and rescue Bonnet.

Now the Charles Town citizens saw that they

must again act for themselves, and not depend upon the home government. If there were pirates outside the harbor, they must be met and fought before they could come up to the city; and the Governor and the Council decided immediately to fit out a little fleet. Four merchant vessels were quickly provided with cannon, ammunition, and men, and the command of this expedition would undoubtedly have been given to Mr. Rhett had it not been that he and the Governor had quarrelled. There being no naval officers in Charles Town, their fighting vessels had to be commanded by civilians, and Governor Johnson now determined that he would try his hand at carrying on a sea-fight. Mr. Rhett had done very well; why should not he?

Before the Governor's little fleet of vessels, one of which was the *Royal James*, captured from Bonnet, was quite ready to sail, the Governor received news that his preparations had not been made a moment too soon, for already two vessels, one a large ship, and the other an armed sloop, had come into the outer harbor, and were lying at anchor off Sullivan's Island. It was very likely that Moody, having returned from some outside operation, was waiting there for the arrival of other pirate ships, and that it was an important thing to attack him at once.

As it was very desirable that the pirates should

not be frightened away before the Charles Town
fleet could reach them, the vessels of the latter were
made to look as much like mere merchantmen as
possible. Their cannon were covered, and the
greater part of the crews was kept below, out of
sight. Thus the four ships came sailing down the
bay, and early in the morning made their appearance in the sight of the pirates. When the ship
and the big sloop saw the four merchant vessels
sailing quietly out of the harbor, they made immediate preparations to capture them. Anchors were
weighed, sails were set, and with a black flag flying
from the topmast of each vessel, the pirates steered
toward the Charles Town fleet, and soon approached
near enough to the *King William*, which was the
foremost of the fleet, to call upon her captain to
surrender. But at that moment Governor Johnson,
who was on board the *Mediterranean*, and could hear
the insolent pirate shouting through his speaking-
trumpet, gave a preconcerted signal. Instantly
everything was changed. The covers were jerked
off from the cannon of the pretended merchantmen,
armed men poured up out of the holds, the flag of
England was quickly raised on each one of them,
and the sixty-eight guns of the combined fleet
opened fire upon the astonished pirates.

The ship which seemed to be the more formidable of the enemy's vessels had run up so close to

her intended prey that two of Governor Johnson's vessels, the *Sea-Nymph* and the *Royal James*, once so bitterly opposed to each other, but now fighting together in honest comradeship, were able to go between her and the open sea and so cut off her retreat.

But if the captain of the pirate ship could not get away, he showed that he was very well able to fight, and although the two vessels which had made him the object of their attack were pouring cannon balls and musket shot upon him, he blazed away with his cannon and his muskets. The three vessels were so near each other that sometimes their yard-arms almost touched, so that this terrible fight seemed almost like a hand-to-hand conflict. For four hours the roaring of the cannon, the crushing of timbers, the almost continuous discharge of musketry were kept up, while the smoke of the battle frequently almost prevented the crews of the contending ships from seeing each other. Not so very far away the people of Charles Town, who were standing on the shores of their beautiful harbor, could see the fierce fight which was going on, and great was the excitement and anxiety throughout the city.

But the time came when two ships grew too much for one, and as the *Royal James* and the *Sea-Nymph* were able to take positions by which they could rake the deck of the pirate vessel, many of her men gave up the fight and rushed down into the hold to save their lives. Then both the Charles Town vessels bore down upon the pirate and boarded her, and now there was another savage battle with pistols and cutlasses. The pirate captain and several of his crew were still on deck, and they fought like wounded lions, and it was not until they had all been cut down or shot that victory came to the men of Charles Town.

Very soon after this terrible battle was over the waiting crowds in the city saw a glorious sight; the pirate ship came sailing slowly up the harbor, a captured vessel, with the *Sea-Nymph* on one side and the *Royal James* on the other, the colors of the Crown flying from the masts of each one of the three.

The other pirate ship, which was quite large, seemed to be more fortunate than her companion, for she was able to get out to sea, and spreading all her sails she made every effort to escape. Governor Johnson, however, had no idea of letting her get away if he could help it. When a civilian goes out to fight a sea-battle he naturally wants to show what he can do, and Governor Johnson did not mean to let people think that Mr. Rhett was a better naval commander than he was. He ordered the *Mediterranean* and the *King William* to put on all sail, and away they went after the big ship. The retreating pirates did everything they could to effect

escape, throwing over their cannon, and even their
boats, in order to lighten their ship, but it was of no
use. The Governor's vessels were the faster sailers,
and when the *King William* got near enough to fire
a few cannon balls into the flying ship, the latter
hauled down the black flag and without hesitation
lay to and surrendered.

It was plain enough that this ship was not manned
by desperate pirates, and when Governor Johnson
went on board of her he found her to be not really
a pirate ship, but an English vessel which not long
before had been captured by the pirates in whose
company she had visited Charles Town harbor.
She had been bringing over from England a company of convicts and what were called "covenant
servants," who were going to the colonies to be disposed of to the planters for a term of years.
Among these were thirty-six women, and when the
South Carolinians went below they were greatly
surprised to find the hold crowded with these unfortunate creatures, some of whom were nearly frightened to death. At the time of this vessel's capture
the pirate captain had enlisted some of the convicts
into his crew, as he needed men, and putting on
board of his prize a few pirates to command her,
the ship had been worked by such of her own crew
and passengers as were willing to serve under
pirates, while the others were shut up below.

Here was a fine prize taken with very little trouble, and the *King William* and the *Mediterranean* returned to Charles Town with their captured ship, to be met with the shouts and cheers of the delighted citizens, already excited to a high pitch by the previous arrival of the captured pirate sloop.

But Governor Johnson met with something else which made a stronger impression on him than the cheers of his townspeople, and this was the great surprise of finding that he had not fought and conquered the pirate Moody; without suspecting such a thing, he had crushed and utterly annihilated the dreaded Worley, whose deeds had created such a consternation in northern waters, and whose threatened approach had sent a thrill of excitement all down the coast. When this astonishing news became known, the flags of the city were waved more wildly, and the shouts and cheers rose higher.

Thus came to an end, in the short time of six weeks, the career of Richard Worley, who, without doubt, did more piratical work in less time than any sea-robber on record.

# Chapter XXVIII

## The Story of Two Women Pirates

THE history of the world gives us many instances of women who have taken the parts of men, almost always acquitting themselves with as much credit as if they had really belonged to the male sex, and, in our modern days, these instances are becoming more frequent than ever before. Joan of Arc put on a suit of armor and bravely led an army, and there have been many other fighting women who made a reputation for themselves ; but it is very seldom that we hear of a woman who became a pirate. There were, however, two women pirates who made themselves very well known on our coast.

The most famous of these women pirates was named Mary Reed. Her father was an English captain of a trading vessel, and her mother sailed with him. This mother had had an elder child, a son, and she also had a mother-in-law in England from whom she expected great things for her little boy. But the boy died, and Mrs. Reed, being afraid that her mother-in-law would not be willing to leave any property to a girl, determined to play a little trick, and make believe that her second child was also a boy.

Consequently, as soon as the little girl, who, from her birth had been called Mary by her father and mother, was old enough to leave off baby clothes, she put on boy's clothes, and when the family returned to England a nice little boy appeared before his grandmother; but all this deception amounted to nothing, for the old lady died without leaving anything to the pretended boy. Mary's mother believed that her child would get along better in the world as a boy than she would as a girl, and therefore she still dressed her in masculine clothes, and put her out to service as a foot-boy, or one of those youngsters who now go by the name of " Buttons."

But Mary did not fancy blacking boots and running errands. She was very well satisfied to be a boy, but she wanted to live the kind of a boy's life which would please her fancy, and as she thought life on the ocean wave would suit her very well, she ran away from her employer's house and enlisted on board a man-of-war as a powder monkey.

After a short time, Mary found that the ocean was not all that she expected it to be, and when she had grown up so that she looked like a good strapping fellow, she ran away from the man-of-war when it was in an English port, and went to Flanders, and there she thought she would try something new, and see whether or not she would like a soldier's life better than that of a sailor. She enlisted in a regiment of foot, and in the course of time she became a very good soldier and took part in several battles, firing her musket and charging with her bayonet as well as any of the men beside her.

But there is a great deal of hard work connected with infantry service, and although she was eager for the excitement of battle with the exhilarating smell of powder and the cheering shouts of her fellow-soldiers, Mary did not fancy tramping on long marches, carrying her heavy musket and knapsack. She got herself changed into a regiment of cavalry, and here, mounted upon a horse, with the encumbrances she disliked to carry comfortably strapped behind her, Mary felt much more at ease, and much better satisfied. But she was not destined to achieve fame as a dashing cavalry man with foaming steed and flashing sabre. One of her comrades was a very prepossessing young fellow, and Mary fell in love with him, and when she told him she was not really a cavalry man but a cavalry woman, he returned her affection, and the two agreed that they would quit the army, and set up domestic life as quiet civilians. They were married, and went into the tavern-keeping business. They were both

fond of horses, and did not wish to sever all connection with the method of life they had just given
up, and so they called their little inn the Three
Horse Shoes, and were always glad when any one
of their customers came riding up to their stables,
instead of simply walking in their door.

But this domestic life did not last very long.
Mary's husband died, and, not wishing to keep a
tavern by herself, she again put on the dress of a
man and enlisted as a soldier. But her military
experience did not satisfy her, and after all she
believed that she liked the sea better than the land,
and again she shipped as a sailor on a vessel bound
for the West Indies.

Now Mary's desire for change and variety seemed
likely to be fully satisfied. The ship was taken by
English pirates, and as she was English and looked
as if she would make a good freebooter, they compelled her to join them, and thus it was that she got
her first idea of a pirate's life. When this company
disbanded, she went to New Providence and enlisted
on a privateer, but, as was very common on such vessels commissioned to perform acts of legal piracy, the
crew soon determined that illegal piracy was much
preferable, so they hoisted the black flag, and began
to scourge the seas.

Mary Reed was now a regular pirate, with a cutlass, pistol, and every outward appearance of a dar-

ing sea-robber, except that she wore no bristling beard, but as her face was sunburned and seamed by the weather, she looked mannish enough to frighten the senses out of any unfortunate trader on whose deck she bounded in company with her shouting, hairy-faced companions. It is told of her that she did not fancy the life of a pirate, but she seemed to believe in the principle of whatever is worth doing is worth doing well; she was as ready with her cutlass and her pistol as any other ocean bandit.

But although Mary was a daring pirate, she was also a woman, and again she fell in love. A very pleasant and agreeable sailor was taken prisoner by the crew of her ship, and Mary concluded that she would take him as her portion of the spoils. Consequently, at the first port they touched she became again a woman and married him, and as they had no other present method of livelihood he remained with her on her ship. Mary and her husband had no real love for a pirate's life, and they determined to give it up as soon as possible, but the chance to do so did not arrive. Mary had a very high regard for her new husband, who was a quiet, amiable man, and not at all suited to his present life, and as he had become a pirate for the love of her, she did everything she could to make life easy for him.

She even went so far as to fight a duel in his place, one of the crew having insulted him, probably thinking him a milksop who would not resent an affront. But the latent courage of Mary's husband instantly blazed up, and he challenged the insulter to a duel. Although Mary thought her husband was brave enough to fight anybody, she thought that perhaps, in some ways, he was a milksop and did not understand the use of arms nearly as well as she did. Therefore, she made him stay on board the ship while she went to a little island near where they were anchored and fought the duel with sword and pistol. The man pirate and the woman pirate now went savagely to work, and it was not long before the man pirate lay dead upon the sand, while Mary returned to an admiring crew and a grateful husband.

During her piratical career Mary fell in with another woman pirate, Anne Bonny, by name, and these women, being perhaps the only two of their kind, became close friends. Anne came of a good family. She was the daughter of an Irish lawyer, who went to Carolina and became a planter, and there the little girl grew up. When her mother died she kept the house, but her disposition was very much more masculine than feminine. She was very quick-tempered and easily enraged, and it is told of her that when an Englishwoman, who was working as a servant in her father's house, had irritated Anne by some carelessness or impertinence, that hot-tempered young woman sprang upon her and stabbed her with a carving-knife.

It is not surprising that Anne soon showed a dislike for the humdrum life on a plantation, and meeting with a young sailor, who owned nothing in the world but the becoming clothes he wore, she married him. Thereupon her father, who seems to have been as hot-headed as his daughter, promptly turned her out of doors. The fiery Anne was glad enough to adopt her husband's life, and she went to sea with him, sailing to New Providence. There she was thrown into an entirely new circle of society. Pirates were in the habit of congregating at this place, and Anne was greatly delighted with the company of these daring, dashing sea-robbers, of whose exploits she had so often heard. The more she associated with the pirates, the less she cared for the plain, stupid sailors, who were content with the merchant service, and she finally deserted her husband and married a Captain Rackham, one of the most attractive and dashing pirates of the day.

Anne went on board the ship of her pirate husband, and as she was sure his profession would exactly suit her wild and impetuous nature, she determined also to become a pirate. She put on man's clothes, girded to her side a cutlass, and hung

pistols in her belt.    During many voyages Anne
sailed with Captain Rackham, and wherever there
was pirate's work to do, she was on deck to do it.
At last the gallant captain came to grief.   He was
captured and condemned to death.   Now there was
an opportunity for Anne's nature to assert itself,
and it did, but it was a very different sort of nature
from that of Mary Reed.   Just before his execution Anne was admitted to see her husband, but
instead of offering to do anything that might comfort him or palliate his dreadful misfortune, she
simply stood and contemptuously glared at him.
She was sorry, she said, to see him in such a predicament, but she told him plainly that if he had
had the courage to fight like a man, he would not
then be waiting to be hung like a dog, and with
that she walked away and left him.

On the occasion when Captain Rackham had
been captured, Mary Reed and her husband were
on board his ship, and there was, perhaps, some
reason for Anne's denunciation of the cowardice
of Captain Rackham.   As has been said, the two
women were good friends and great fighters, and
when they found the vessel engaged in a fight with
a man-of-war, they stood together upon the deck
and boldly fought, although the rest of the crew,
and even the captain himself, were so discouraged
by the heavy fire which was brought to bear on
them, that they had retreated to the hold.

Mary and Anne were so disgusted at this exhibition of cowardice, that they rushed to the hatchways and shouted to their dastardly companions to come up and help defend the ship, and when their entreaties were disregarded they were so enraged that they fired down into the hold, killing one of the frightened pirates and wounding several others. But their ship was taken, and Mary and Anne, in company with all the pirates who had been left alive, were put in irons and carried to England.

When she was in prison, Mary declared that she and her husband had firmly intended to give up piracy and become private citizens. But when she was put on trial, the accounts of her deeds had a great deal more effect than her words upon her judges, and she was condemned to be executed. She was saved, however, from this fate by a fever of which she died soon after her conviction.

The impetuous Anne was also condemned, but the course of justice is often very curious and difficult to understand, and this hard-hearted and sanguinary woman was reprieved and finally pardoned. Whether or not she continued to disport herself as a man we do not know, but it is certain that she was the last of the female pirates.

There are a great many things which women can do as well as men, and there are many professions and lines of work from which they have been long

debarred, and for which they are most admirably
adapted, but it seems to me that piracy is not one
of them.    It is said that a woman's nature is apt to
carry her too far, and I have never heard of any man
pirate who would allow himself to become so enraged against the cowardice of his companions that
he would deliberately fire down into the hold of
a vessel containing his wife and a crowd of his
former associates.

## Chapter XXIX

### A Pirate from Boyhood

ABOUT the beginning of the eighteenth century there lived in Westminster, England, a boy who very early in life made a choice of a future career. Nearly all boys have ideas upon this subject, and while some think they would like to be presidents or generals of armies, others fancy that they would prefer to be explorers of unknown countries or to keep candy shops. But it generally happens that these youthful ideas are never carried out, and that the boy who would wish to sell candy because he likes to eat it, becomes a farmer on the western prairie, where confectionery is never seen, and the would-be general determines to study for the ministry.

But Edward Low, the boy under consideration, was a different sort of a fellow. The life of a robber suited his youthful fancy, and he not only adopted it at a very early age, but he stuck to it until the end of his life. He was much stronger and bolder than the youngsters with whom he associated, and

he soon became known among them as a regular
land pirate. If a boy possessed anything which
Ned Low desired, whether it happened to be an
apple, a nut, or a farthing, the young robber gave
chase to him, and treated him as a pirate treats a
merchant vessel which he has boarded.

Not only did young Low resemble a pirate in
his dishonest methods, but he also resembled one
in his meanness and cruelty; if one of his victims was supposed by him to have hidden any of
the treasures which his captor believed him to possess, Low would inflict upon him every form of
punishment which the ingenuity of a bad boy could
devise, in order to compel him to confess where he
had concealed the half-penny which had been given
to him for holding a horse, or the ball with which
he had been seen playing. In the course of time
this young street pirate became a terror to all boys
in that part of London in which he lived, and by
beginning so early he acquired a great proficiency
in dishonest and cruel practices.

It is likely that young Low inherited his knavish
disposition, for one of his brothers became a very
bold and ingenious thief, and invented a new kind
of robbery which afterwards was popular in London.
This brother grew to be a tall fellow, and it was his
practice to dress himself like a porter, — one of
those men who in those days carried packages and

parcels about the city. On his head he poised a
basket, and supporting this burden with his hands,
he hurriedly made his way through the most crowded
streets of London.

The basket was a heavy one, but it did not con-
tain any ordinary goods, such as merchandise or
marketing; but instead of these it held a very sharp
and active boy seven years old, one of the younger
members of the Low family. As the tall brother
pushed rapidly here and there among the hurrying
people on the sidewalks, the boy in the basket would
suddenly stretch out with his wiry young arm, and
snatch the hat or the wig of some man who might
pass near enough for him to reach him. This done,
the porter and his basket would quickly be lost in the
crowd; and even if the astonished citizen, suddenly
finding himself hatless and wigless, beheld the long-
legged Low, he would have no reason to suppose that
that industrious man with the basket on his head
had anything to do with the loss of his head covering.

This new style of street robbery must have been
quite profitable, for of course the boy in the basket
was well instructed, and never snatched at a shabby
hat or a poor looking wig. The elder Low came
to have a good many imitators, and it happened
in the course of time that many a worthy citizen of
London wished there were some harmless way of
gluing his wig to the top of his head, or that it

were the custom to secure the hat by means of strings tied under the chin.

As Ned Low grew up to be a strong young fellow, he also grew discontented with the pilferings and petty plunders which were possible to him in the London streets, and so he went to sea and sailed to America. He landed in Boston, and, as it was necessary to work in order to eat, — for opportunities of a dishonest livelihood had not yet opened themselves before him, — he undertook to learn the trade of a rigger, but as he was very badly suited to any sort of steady occupation, he soon quarrelled with his master, ran away, and got on board a vessel bound for Honduras.

For a time he earned a livelihood by cutting logwood, but it was not long before he quarrelled with the captain of the vessel for whom he was working, and finally became so enraged that he tried to kill him. He did not succeed in this dastardly attempt, but as he could not commit murder he decided to do the next worst thing, and so gathering together twelve of the greatest rascals among his companions, they seized a boat, went out to the captain's schooner, which was lying near shore, and took possession of it. Then they hoisted anchor, ran up the sail, and put out to sea, leaving the captain and the men who were with him to take care of themselves the best that they could and live on logwood leaves if they could find nothing else to eat.

Now young Low was out upon the ocean in possession of a vessel and in command of twelve sturdy scoundrels, and he did not have the least trouble in the world in making up his mind what he should do next. As soon as he could manufacture a black flag from materials he found on board, he flung this ominous ensign to the breeze, and declared himself a pirate. This was the summit of his ambition, and in this new profession he had very little to learn. From a boy thief to a man pirate the way is easy enough.

The logwood schooner, of course, was not provided with the cannon, cutlasses, and pistols necessary for piratical undertakings, and therefore Low found himself in the position of a young man beginning business with a very small capital. So, in the hopes of providing himself with the necessary appliances for his work, Low sailed for one of the islands of the West Indies which was a resort for pirates, and there he had very good fortune, for he fell in with a man named Lowther who was already well established in the profession of piracy.

When Low sailed into the little port with his home-made black flag floating above him, Lowther received him with the greatest courtesy and hospitality, and shortly afterwards proposed to the newly fledged pirate to go into partnership with him. This offer was accepted, and Low was made second

in command of the little fleet of two vessels, each
of which was well provided with arms, ammunition,
and all things necessary for robbery on the high
seas.

The partnership between these two rascals did
not continue very long. They took several valua-
able prizes, and the more booty he obtained, the
higher became Low's opinion of himself, and the
greater his desire for independent action. Therefore it was that when they had captured a large
brigantine, Low determined that he would no longer
serve under any man. He made a bargain with
Lowther by which they dissolved partnership, and
Low became the owner of the brigantine. In this
vessel, with forty-four men as a crew, he again started
out in the black flag business on his own account,
and parting from his former chief officer, he sailed
northward.

As Low had landed in Boston, and had lived some
time in that city, he seems to have conceived a fancy
for New England, which, however, was not at all re-
ciprocated by the inhabitants of that part of the
country.

Among the first feats which Low performed in
New England waters was the capture of a sloop
about to enter one of the ports of Rhode Island.
When he had taken everything out of this vessel
which he wanted, Low cut away the yards from the

masts and stripped the vessel of all its sails and rigging. As his object was to get away from these waters before his presence was discovered by the people on shore, he not only made it almost impossible to sail the vessel he had despoiled, but he wounded the captain and others of the peaceful crew so that they should not be able to give information to any passing craft. Then he sailed away as rapidly as possible in the direction of the open sea. In spite, however, of all the disadvantages under which they labored, the crew of the merchant vessel managed to get into Block Island, and from there a small boat was hurriedly rowed over to Rhode Island, carrying intelligence of the bold piracy which had been committed so close to one of its ports.

When the Governor heard what had happened, he quickly sent out drummers to sound the alarm in the seaport towns and to call upon volunteers to go out and capture the pirates. So great was the resentment caused by the audacious deed of Low that a large number of volunteers hastened to offer their services to the Governor, and two vessels were fitted out with such rapidity that, although their commanders had only heard of the affair in the morning, they were ready to sail before sunset. They put on all sail and made the best speed they could, and although they really caught sight of Low's ship, the pirate vessel was a swifter craft than those in pursuit of her, and the angry sailors of Rhode Island were at last compelled to give up the chase.

The next of Low's transactions was on a wholesale scale. Rounding Cape Cod and sailing up the coast, he at last reached the vicinity of Marblehead, and there, in a harbor called in those days Port Rosemary, he found at anchor a fleet of thirteen merchant vessels. This was a grand sight, as welcome to the eye of a pirate as a great nugget of gold would be to a miner who for weary days had been washing yellow grains from the "pay dirt" which he had laboriously dug from the hard soil.

It would have been easy for Low to take his pick from these vessels quietly resting in the little harbor, for he soon perceived that none of them were armed nor were they able to protect themselves from assault, but his audacity was of an expansive kind, and he determined to capture them all. Sailing boldly into the harbor, he hoisted the dreadful black flag, and then, standing on his quarter-deck with his speaking-trumpet, he shouted to each vessel as he passed it that if it did not surrender he would board it and give no quarter to captain or crew. Of course there was nothing else for the peaceful sailors to do but to submit, and so this greedy pirate took possession of each vessel in turn and stripped it of everything of value he cared to take away.

But he did not confine himself to stealing the goods on board these merchantmen. As he preferred to command several vessels instead of one, he took possession of some of the best of the ships and compelled as many of their men as he thought he would need to enter his service. Then, as one of the captured vessels was larger and better than his brigantine, he took it for his own ship, and at the head of the little pirate fleet he bid farewell to Marblehead and started out on a grand cruise against the commerce of our coast.

It is wonderful how rapidly this man Low succeeded in his business enterprises. Beginning with a little vessel with a dozen unarmed men, he found himself in a very short time at the head of what was perhaps the largest piratical force in American waters. What might have happened if Nature had not taken a hand in this game it is not difficult to imagine, for our seaboard towns, especially those of the South, would have been an easy prey to Low and his fleet.

But sailing down to the West Indies, probably in order to fit out his ships with guns, arms, and ammunition before beginning a naval campaign, his fleet was overtaken by a terrible storm, and in order to save the vessels they were obliged to throw overboard a great many of the heavier goods they had captured at Marblehead, and when at last they found

shelter in the harbor of a small island, they were glad
that they had escaped with their lives.

The grasping and rapacious Low was not now in
a condition to proceed to any rendezvous of pirates
where he might purchase the arms and supplies he
needed.  A great part of his valuable plunder had
gone to the bottom of the sea, and he was therefore
obliged to content himself with operations upon a
comparatively small scale.

How small and contemptible this scale was it is
scarcely possible for an ordinary civilized being to
comprehend, but the soul of this ignoble pirate was
capable of extraordinary baseness.

When he had repaired the damage to his ships,
Low sailed out from the island, and before long he
fell in with a wrecked vessel which had lost all its
masts in a great storm, and was totally disabled,
floating about wherever the winds chose to blow it.
The poor fellows on board greatly needed succor,
and there is no doubt that when they saw the
approach of sails their hopes rose high, and even if
they had known what sort of ships they were which
were making their way toward them, they would
scarcely have suspected that the commander of
these goodly vessels was such an utterly despicable
scoundrel as he proved to be.

Instead of giving any sort of aid to the poor
shipwrecked crew, Low and his men set to work

to plunder their vessel, and they took from it a thousand pounds in money, and everything of value which they could find on board. Having thus stripped the unfortunate wreck, they departed, leaving the captain and crew of the disabled vessel to perish by storm or starvation, unless some other vessel, manned by human beings and not pitiless beasts, should pass their way and save them.

Low now commenced a long series of piratical depredations. He captured many merchantmen, he committed the vilest cruelties upon his victims, and in every way proved himself to be one of the meanest and most black-hearted pirates of whom we have any account. It is not necessary to relate his various dastardly performances. They were all very much of the same order, and none of them possessed any peculiar interest; his existence is referred to in these pages because he was one of the most noted and successful pirates of his time, and also because his career indicated how entirely different was the character of the buccaneers of previous days from that of the pirates who in the eighteenth century infested our coast. The first might have been compared to bold and dashing highwaymen, who at least showed courage and daring; but the others resembled sneak thieves, always seeking to commit a crime if they could do it in safety, but never willing to risk their cowardly necks in any danger.

The buccaneers of the olden days were certainly men of the greatest bravery. They did not hesitate to attack well-armed vessels manned by crews much larger than their own, and in later periods they faced cannon and conquered cities. Their crimes were many and vile; but when they committed cruelties they did so in order to compel their prisoners to disclose their hidden treasures, and when they attacked a Spanish vessel, and murdered all on board, they had in their hearts the remembrance that the Spanish naval forces gave no quarter to buccaneers.

But pirates such as Edward Low showed not one palliating feature in their infamous characters. To rob and desert a shipwrecked crew was only one of Low's contemptible actions. It appears that he seldom attacked a vessel from which there seemed to be any probability of resistance, and we read of no notable combats or sea-fights in which he was engaged. He preyed upon the weak and defenceless, and his inhuman cruelties were practised, not for the sake of extorting gain from his victims, but simply to gratify his spite and love of wickedness.

There were men among Low's followers who looked upon him as a bold and brave leader, for he was always a blusterer and a braggart, and there were honest seamen and merchants who were very much afraid of him, but time proved that there was no reason for any one to suppose that Edward Low had a spark of courage in his composition. He was brave enough when he was attacking an unarmed crew, but when he had to deal with any vessel capable of inflicting any injury upon him he was a coward indeed.

Sailing in company with one companion vessel, — for he had discarded the greater part of his pirate fleet, — Low sighted a good-sized ship at a considerable distance, and he and his consort immediately gave chase, supposing the distant vessel might prove to be a good prize. It so happened, however, that the ship discovered by Low was an English man-of-war, the *Greyhound*, which was cruising along the coast looking for these very pirates, who had recently committed some outrageous crimes upon the crews of merchant vessels in those waters.

When the two ships, with the black flags floating above them and their decks crowded with desperate fellows armed with pistols and cutlasses, drew near to the vessel, of which they expected to make a prize, they were greatly amazed when she suddenly turned in her course and delivered a broadside from her heavy cannon. The pirates returned the fire, for they were well armed with cannon, and there was nothing else for them to do but fight, but the combat was an extremely short one. Low's consort was soon disabled by the fire from the man-of-war, and, as soon as he perceived this, the dastardly

Low, without any regard for his companions in arms, and with no thought for anything but his own safety, immediately stopped fighting, and setting all sail, sped away from the scene of combat as swiftly as it was possible for the wind to force his vessel through the water.

The disabled pirate ship was quickly captured, and not long afterwards twenty-five of her crew were tried, convicted, and hung near Newport, Rhode Island. But the arrant Low escaped without injury, and continued his career of contemptible crime for some time longer. What finally became of him is not set down in the histories of piracy. It is not improbable that if the men under his command were not too brutally stupid to comprehend his cowardly unfaithfulness to them, they suddenly removed from this world one of the least interesting of all base beings.

# Chapter XXX

## The Pirate of the Gulf

AT the beginning of this century there was a very able and, indeed, talented man living on the shores of the Gulf of Mexico, who has been set down in the historical records of the times as a very important pirate, and who is described in story and in tradition as a gallant and romantic freebooter of the sea. This man was Jean Lafitte, widely known as "The Pirate of the Gulf," and yet who was, in fact, so little of a pirate, that it may be doubted whether or not he deserves a place in these stories of American pirates.

Lafitte was a French blacksmith, and, while still a young man, he came with his two brothers to New Orleans, and set up a shop in Bourbon Street, where he did a good business in horseshoeing and in other branches of his trade. But he had a soul which soared high above his anvil and his bellows, and perceiving an opportunity to take up a very profitable occupation, he gave up blacksmithing, and with his two brothers as partners became a super-

intendent of privateering and a general manager
of semi-legalized piracy. The business opportunity
which came to the watchful and clear-sighted Lafitte
may be briefly described.

In the early years of this century the Gulf of
Mexico was the scene of operations of small vessels
calling themselves privateers, but in fact pirates.
War had broken out between England and Spain,
on the one side, and France on the other, and consequently the first-named nations were very glad to commission privateers to prey upon the commerce of
France. There were also privateers who had been
sent out by some of the Central American republics
who had thrown off the Spanish yoke, and these,
considering Spanish vessels as their proper booty,
were very much inclined to look upon English
vessels in the same light, as the English and
Spanish were allies. And when a few French privateers came also upon the scene, they helped to
make the business of legitimate capture of merchantmen, during the time of war, a very complicated
affair.

But upon one point these privateers, who so
often acted as pirates, because they had not the
spare time in which to work out difficult problems
of nationality, were all agreed: when they had
loaded their ships with booty, they must sail to
some place where it would be safe to dispose of it.

So, in course of time, the bay of Barrataria, about forty miles south of New Orleans and very well situated for an illegal settlement, was chosen as a privateers' port, and a large and flourishing colony soon grew up at the head of the bay, to which came privateers of every nationality to dispose of their cargoes.

Of course there was no one in the comparatively desolate country about Barrataria who could buy the valuable goods which were brought into that port, but the great object of the owners of this merchandise was to smuggle it up to New Orleans and dispose of it. But there could be no legitimate traffic of this sort, for the United States at the very beginning of the century was at peace with England, France, and Spain, and therefore could not receive into any of her ports, goods which had been captured from the ships of these nations. Consequently the plunder of the privateering pirates of Barrataria was brought up to New Orleans in all sorts of secret and underhand fashions, and sold to merchants in that city, without the custom house having anything to do with the importations.

Now this was great business; Jean Lafitte had a great business mind, and therefore it was not long after his arrival at Barrataria before he was the head man in the colony, and director-in-chief of all its operations. Thus, by becoming a prominent

figure in a piratical circle, he came to be considered
a pirate, and as such came down to us in the pages
of history.

But, in fact, Lafitte never committed an act of
piracy in his life; he was a blacksmith, and knew
no more about sailing a ship or even the smallest
kind of a boat than he knew about the proper construction of a sonnet. He did not even try, like the
celebrated Bonnet, to find other people who would
navigate a vessel for him, for he had no taste for the
ocean wave, and all that he had to do he did upon
firm, dry land. It is said of him that he was never
at sea but twice in his life: once when he came from
France, and once when he left this country, and on
neither occasion did he sail under the " Jolly Roger,"
as the pirate flag was sometimes called. For these
reasons it seems scarcely right to call Lafitte a pirate,
but as he has been so generally considered in that
light, we will admit him into the bad company, the
stories of whose lives we are now telling.

The energy and business abilities of Jean Lafitte
soon made themselves felt not only in Barrataria,
but in New Orleans. The privateers found that he
managed their affairs with much discretion and considerable fairness, and, while they were willing to
depend upon him, they were obliged to obey him.

On the other hand, the trade of New Orleans was
very much influenced by the great quantities of

goods which under Lafitte's directions were smuggled into the city. Many merchants and shopkeepers who possessed no consciences to speak of were glad to buy these smuggled goods for very little money and to sell them at low prices and large profits, but the respectable business men, who were obliged to pay market prices for their goods, were greatly disturbed by the large quantities of merchandise which were continually smuggled into New Orleans and sold at rates with which they could not compete.

It was toward the end of our war with England, which began in 1812, that the government of the United States, urged to speedy action by the increasing complaints of the law-abiding merchants of New Orleans, determined to send out a small naval force and entirely break up the illegitimate rendezvous at Barrataria.

Lafitte's two brothers were in New Orleans acting as his agents, and one of them, Dominique, was arrested and thrown into prison, and Commodore Patterson, who was commanding at that station, was ordered to fit out an expedition as quickly as possible to sail down to Barrataria to destroy the ships found in the bay, to capture the town, and to confiscate and seize upon all goods which might be found in the place.

When Jean Lafitte heard of the vigorous methods which were about to be taken against him, his prospects must have been very gloomy ones, for of course he could not defend his little colony against a regular naval force, which, although its large vessels could not sail into the shallow bay, could send out boats with armed crews against which it would be foolish for him to contend. But just about this time a very strange thing happened.

A strong English naval force had taken possession of Pensacola, Florida, and as an attack upon New Orleans was contemplated, the British commander, knowing of Lafitte's colony at Barrataria, and believing that these hardy and reckless adventurers would be very valuable allies in the proposed movement upon the city, determined to send an ambassador to Lafitte to see what could be done in the way of forming an alliance with this powerful leader of semi-pirates and smugglers.

Accordingly, the sloop of war *Sophia*, commanded by Captain Lockyer, was sent to Barrataria to treat with Lafitte, and when this vessel arrived off the mouth of the harbor, which she could not enter, she began firing signal guns in order to attract the attention of the people of the colony. Naturally enough, the report of the *Sophia's* guns created a great excitement in Barrataria, and all the people who happened to be at the settlement at that time crowded out upon the beach to see what they could see. But the war-vessel was too far away for them to distinguish her nationality, and Lafitte quickly made up his mind that the only thing for him to do was to row out to the mouth of the harbor and see what was the matter. Without doubt he feared that this was the United States vessel which had come to break up his settlement. But whether this was the case or not, he must go out and try the effect of fair words, for he had no desire whatever to defend his interests by hard blows.

Before Lafitte reached the vessel he was surprised to find it was a British man-of-war, not an American, and very soon he saw that a boat was coming from it and rowing toward him. This boat contained Captain Lockyer and two other officers, besides the men who rowed it; when the two boats met, the captain told who he was, and asked if Mr. Lafitte could be found in Barrataria, stating that he had an important document to deliver to him. The cautious Frenchman did not immediately admit that he was the man for whom the document was intended, but he said that Lafitte was at Barrataria, and as the two boats rowed together toward shore, he thought it would be as well to announce his position, and did so.

When the crowd of privateersmen saw the officers in British uniform landing upon their beach, they were not inclined to receive them kindly, for an attack had been made upon the place by a small

British force some time before, and a good deal of
damage had been done.    But Lafitte quieted the
angry feelings of his followers, conducted the officers
to his own house, and treated them with great hospitality, which he was able to do in fine style, for
his men brought into Barrataria luxuries from all
parts of the world.

When Lafitte opened the package of papers which
Captain Lockyer handed to him, he was very much
surprised.    Some of them were general proclamations announcing the intention of Great Britain if
the people of Louisiana did not submit to her demands ; but the most important document was one
in which Colonel Nichols, commander-in-chief of
the British forces in the Gulf, made an offer to
Lafitte and his followers to become a part of the
British navy, promising to give amnesty to all the
inhabitants of Barrataria, to make their leader a
captain in the navy, and to do a great many other
good things, provided they would join his forces, and
help him to attack the American seaports.    In case,
however, this offer should be refused, the Barrata-
rians were assured that their place would speedily
be attacked, their vessels destroyed, and all their
possessions confiscated.

Lafitte was now in a state of great perplexity.
He did not wish to become a British captain, for
his knowledge of horseshoeing would be of no ser-

vice to him in such a capacity; moreover, he had
no love for the British, and his sympathies were
all on the side of the United States in this war.
But here he was with the British commander asking him to become an ally, and to take up arms
against the United States, threatening at the same
time to destroy him and his colony in case of re-
fusal.   On the other hand, there was the United
States at that moment preparing an expedition
for the purpose of breaking up the settlement at
Barrataria, and to do everything which the British
threatened to do, in case Lafitte did not agree to
their proposals.

The chief of Barrataria might have made a poor
show with a cutlass and a brace of pistols, but he
was a long-headed and sagacious man, with a strong
tendency to practical diplomacy.   He was in a bad
scrape, and he must act with decision and prompt-
ness, if he wanted to get out of it.

The first thing he did was to gain time by delay-
ing his answer to the proposition brought by Captain
Lockyer.   He assured that officer that he must
consult with his people and see what they would do,
and that he must also get rid of some truculent
members of the colony, who would never agree to
act in concert with England, and that therefore he
should not be able to give an answer to Colonel
Nichols for two weeks.   Captain Lockyer saw for

himself that it would not be an easy matter to induce
these independent and unruly fellows, many of whom
already hated England, to enter into the British
service.   Therefore he thought it would be wise to
allow Lafitte the time he asked for, and he sailed
away, promising to return in fifteen days.

The diplomatic Lafitte, having finished for a time
his negotiations with the British, lost no time in
communicating with the American authorities.   He
sent to Governor Claiborne, of Louisiana, all the
documents he had received from Captain Lockyer,
and wrote him a letter in which he told him everything that had happened, and thus gave to the
United States the first authentic information of the
proposed attack upon Mobile and New Orleans.
He then told the Governor that he had no intention
of fighting against the country he had adopted;
that he was perfectly willing and anxious to aid her
in every manner possible, and that he and his followers would gladly join the United States against the
British, asking nothing in return except that all
proceedings against Barrataria should be abandoned,
that amnesty should be given to him and his men,
that his brother should be released from prison,
and that an act of oblivion should be passed by
which the deeds of the smugglers of Barrataria
should be condoned and forgotten.

Furthermore, he said that if the United States

government did not accede to his proposition, he would immediately depart from Barrataria with all his men ; for no matter what loss such a proceeding might prove to him he would not remain in a place where he might be forced to act against the United States. Lafitte also wrote to a member of the Louisiana Legislature, and his letters were well calculated to produce a very good effect in his favor.

The Governor immediately called a council, and submitted the papers and letters received from Lafitte. When these had been read, two points were considered by the council, the first being that the letters and proclamations from the British might be forgeries concocted by Lafitte for the purpose of averting the punishment which was threatened by the United States ; and the second, whether or not it would be consistent with the dignity of the government to treat with this leader of pirates and smugglers.

The consultation resulted in a decision not to have anything to do with Lafitte in the way of negotiations, and to hurry forward the preparations which had been made for the destruction of the dangerous and injurious settlement at Barrataria. In consequence of this action of the council, Commodore Patterson sailed in a very few days down the Mississippi and attacked the pirate settlement at Barrataria with such effect that most of her ships

were taken, many prisoners and much valuable
merchandise captured, and the whole place utterly
destroyed. Lafitte, with the greater part of his
men, had fled to the woods, and so escaped capture.

Captain Lockyer at the appointed time arrived
off the harbor of Barrataria and blazed away with
his signal guns for forty-eight hours, but receiving
no answer, and fearing to send a boat into the
harbor, suspecting treachery on the part of Lafitte,
he was obliged to depart in ignorance of what had
happened.

When the papers and letters which had been sent
to Governor Claiborne by Lafitte were made public,
the people of Louisiana and the rest of the country
did not at all agree with the Governor and his
council in regard to their decision and their subsequent action, and Edward Livingston, a distinguished lawyer of New York, took the part of
Lafitte and argued very strongly in favor of his
loyalty and honesty in the affair.

Even when it was discovered that all the information which Lafitte had sent was perfectly correct,
and that a formidable attack was about to be made
upon New Orleans, General Jackson, who was in
command in that part of the country, issued a very
savage proclamation against the British method of
making war, and among their wicked deeds he mentioned nothing which seemed to him to be worse

than their endeavor to employ against the citizens of the United States the band of "hellish banditti" commanded by Jean Lafitte!

But public opinion was strongly in favor of the ex-pirate of the Gulf, and as things began to look more and more serious in regard to New Orleans, General Jackson was at last very glad, in spite of all that he had said, to accept the renewed offers of Lafitte and his men to assist in the defence of the city, and in consequence of his change of mind many of the former inhabitants of Barrataria fought in the battle of New Orleans and did good work. Their services were so valuable, in fact, that when the war closed President Madison issued a proclamation in which it was stated that the former inhabitants of Barrataria, in consequence of having abandoned their wicked ways of life, and having assisted in the defence of their country, were now granted full pardon for all the evil deeds they had previously committed.

Now Lafitte and his men were free and independent citizens of the United States; they could live where they pleased without fear of molestation, and could enter into any sort of legal business which suited their fancy, but this did not satisfy Lafitte. He had endeavored to take a prompt and honest stand on the side of his country; his offers had been treated with contempt and disbelief; he had been branded as a deceitful knave, and no disposition had been shown to act justly toward him until his services became so necessary to the government that it was obliged to accept them.

Consequently, Lafitte, accompanied by some of his old adherents, determined to leave a country where his loyalty had received such unsatisfactory recognition, and to begin life again in some other part of the American continent. Not long after the war he sailed out upon the Gulf of Mexico, — for what destination it is not known, but probably for some Central American port, — and as nothing was ever heard of him or his party, it is believed by many persons that they all perished in the great storm which arose soon after their departure. There were other persons, however, who stated that he reached Yucatan, where he died on dry land in 1826.

But the end of Lafitte is no more doubtful than his right to the title given to him by people of a romantic turn of mind, and other persons of a still more fanciful disposition might be willing to suppose that the Gulf of Mexico, indignant at the undeserved distinction which had come to him, had swallowed him up in order to put an end to his pretension to the title of "The Pirate of the Gulf."

# Chapter XXXI

## The Pirate of the Buried Treasure

AMONG all the pirates who have figured in history, legend, or song, there is one whose name stands preëminent as the typical hero of the dreaded black flag. The name of this man will instantly rise in the mind of almost every reader, for when we speak of pirates we always think of Captain Kidd.

In fact, however, Captain Kidd was not a typical pirate, for in many ways he was different from the ordinary marine freebooter, especially when we consider him in relation to our own country. All other pirates who made themselves notorious on our coast were known as robbers, pillagers, and ruthless destroyers of life and property, but Captain Kidd's fame was of another kind. We do not think of him as a pirate who came to carry away the property of American citizens, for nearly all the stories about him relate to his arrival at different points on our shores for the sole purpose of burying and thus concealing the rich treasures which he had collected in other parts of the world.

This novel reputation given a pirate who enriched our shore by his deposits and took away none of the possessions of our people could not fail to make Captain Kidd a most interesting personage, and the result has been that he has been lifted out of the sphere of ordinary history and description into the region of imagination and legendary romance. In a word, he has been made a hero of fiction and song. It may be well, then, to assume that there are two Captain Kidds, — one the Kidd of legend and story, and the other the Kidd of actual fact, and we will consider, one at a time, the two characters in which we know the man.

As has been said before, nearly all the stories of the legendary Captain Kidd relate to his visits along our northern coast, and even to inland points, for the purpose of concealing the treasures which had been amassed in other parts of the world.

Thus if we were to find ourselves in almost any village or rural settlement along the coast of New Jersey or Long Island, and were to fall in with any old resident who was fond of talking to strangers, he would probably point out to us the blackened and weather-beaten ribs of a great ship which had been wrecked on the sand bar off the coast during a terrible storm long ago; he would show us where the bathing was pleasant and safe; he would tell us of the best place for fishing, and probably show us the high bluff a little back from the beach from which the Indian maiden leaped to escape the tomahawk of her enraged lover, and then he would be almost sure to tell us of the secluded spot where it was said Captain Kidd and his pirates once buried a lot of treasure.

If we should ask our garrulous guide why this treasure had not been dug up by the people of the place, he would probably shake his head and declare that personally he knew nothing about it, but that it was generally believed that it was there, and he had heard that there had been people who had tried to find it, but if they did find any they never said anything about it, and it was his opinion that if Captain Kidd ever put any gold or silver or precious stones under the ground on that part of the coast these treasures were all there yet.

Further questioning would probably develop the fact that there was a certain superstition which prevented a great many people from interfering with the possible deposits which Captain Kidd had made in their neighborhood, and although few persons would be able to define exactly the foundation of the superstition, it was generally supposed that most of the pirates' treasures were guarded by pirate ghosts. In that case, of course, timid individuals would be

deterred from going out by themselves at night, —
for that was the proper time to dig for buried treasure, — and as it would not have been easy to get
together a number of men each brave enough to
give the others courage, many of the spots reputed
to be the repositories of buried treasure have never
been disturbed.

In spite of the fear of ghosts, in spite of the want
of accurate knowledge in regard to favored localities,
in spite of hardships, previous disappointments, or
expected ridicule, a great many extensive excavations
have been made in the sands or the soil along the
coasts of our northern states, and even in quiet
woods lying miles from the sea, to which it would
have been necessary for the pirates to carry their
goods in wagons, people have dug and hoped and
have gone away sadly to attend to more sensible
business, and far up some of our rivers — where a
pirate vessel never floated — people have dug with
the same hopeful anxiety, and have stopped digging
in the same condition of dejected disappointment.

Sometimes these enterprises were conducted on a
scale which reminds us of the operations on the gold
coast of California. Companies were organized,
stock was issued and subscribed for, and the excavations were conducted under the direction of skilful
treasure-seeking engineers.

It is said that not long ago a company was organ-

ized in Nova Scotia for the purpose of seeking for
Captain Kidd's treasures in a place which it is highly
probable Captain Kidd never saw.  A great excavation having been made, the water from the sea came
in and filled it up, but the work was stopped only
long enough to procure steam pumps with which
the big hole could be drained.  At last accounts the
treasures had not been reached, and this incident is
mentioned only to show how this belief in buried
treasures continues even to the present day.

There is a legend which differs somewhat from
the ordinary run of these stories, and it is told
about a little island on the coast of Cape Cod,
which is called Hannah Screecher's Island, and this
is the way its name came to it.

Captain Kidd while sailing along the coast, looking for a suitable place to bury some treasure, found
this island adapted to his purpose, and landed there
with his savage crew, and his bags and boxes, and
his gold and precious stones.  It was said to be the
habit of these pirates, whenever they made a deposit
on the coast, to make the hole big enough not only
to hold the treasure they wished to deposit there,
but the body of one of the crew, — who was buried
with the valuables in order that his spirit might
act as a day and night watchman to frighten away
people who might happen to be digging in that
particular spot.

The story relates that somewhere on the coast Captain Kidd had captured a young lady named Hannah, and not knowing what to do with her, and desiring not to commit an unnecessary extravagance by disposing of a useful sailor, he determined to kill Hannah, and bury her with the treasure, in order that she might keep away intruders until he came for it.

It was very natural that when Hannah was brought on shore and found out what was going to be done with her, she should screech in a most dreadful manner, and although the pirates soon silenced her and covered her up, they did not succeed in silencing her spirit, and ever since that time, — according to the stories told by some of the older inhabitants of Cape Cod, — there may be heard in the early dusk of the evening the screeches of Hannah coming across the water from her little island to the mainland.

Mr. James Herbert Morse has written a ballad founded upon this peculiar incident, and with the permission of the author we give it here : —

### THE LADY HANNAH.

"Now take my hand," quoth Captain Kidd,
   "The air is blithe, I scent the meads."
He led her up the starlit sands,
   Out of the rustling reeds.

The great white owl then beat his breast,
Athwart the cedars whirred and flew ;
"There's death in our handsome captain's eye,"
Murmured the pirate's crew.

And long they lay upon their oars
And cursed the silence and the chill ;
They cursed the wail of the rising wind,
For no man dared be still.

Of ribald songs they sang a score
To stifle the midnight sobs and sighs,
They told wild tales of the Indian Main,
To drown the far-off cries.

But when they ceased, and Captain Kidd
Came down the sands of Dead Neck Isle,
"My lady wearies," he grimly said,
"And she would rest awhile.

"I've made her a bed — 'tis here, 'tis there,
And she shall wake, be it soon or long,
Where grass is green and wild birds sing
And the wind makes undersong.

"Be quick, my men, and give a hand,
She loved soft furs and silken stuff,
Jewels of gold and silver bars,
And she shall have enough.

"With silver bars and golden ore,
So fine a lady she shall be,
A many suitor shall seek her long,
As they sought Penelope.

" And if a lover would win her hand,
　　No lips e'er kissed a hand so white,
And if a lover would hear her sing,
　　She sings at owlet light.

" But if a lover would win her gold,
　　And his hands be strong to lift the lid,
'Tis here, 'tis there, 'tis everywhere —
　　In the chest," quoth Captain Kidd.

They lifted long, they lifted well,
　　Ingots of gold, and silver bars,
　　And silken plunder from wild, wild wars,
But where they laid them, no man can tell,
　　Though known to a thousand stars.

But the ordinary Kidd stories are very much the same, and depend a good deal upon the character of the coast and upon the imagination of the people who live in that region. We will give one of them as a sample, and from this a number of very good pirate stories could be manufactured by ingenious persons.

It was a fine summer night late in the seventeenth century. A young man named Abner Stout, in company with his wife Mary, went out for a walk upon the beach. They lived in a little village near the coast of New Jersey. Abner was a good carpenter, but a poor man; but he and his wife were very happy with each other, and as they walked toward the sea in the light of the full moon, no young lovers could have been more gay.

When they reached a little bluff covered with low shrubbery, which was the first spot from which they could have a full view of the ocean, Abner suddenly stopped, and pointed out to Mary an unusual sight.   There, as plainly in view as if it had been broad daylight, was a vessel lying at the entrance of the little bay.   The sails were furled, and it was apparently anchored.

For a minute Abner gazed in utter amazement at the sight of this vessel, for no ships, large or small, came to this little lonely bay.   There was a harbor two or three miles farther up the coast to which all trading craft repaired.   What could the strange ship want here?

This unusual visitor to the little bay was a very low and very long, black schooner, with tall masts which raked forward, and with something which looked very much like a black flag fluttering in its rigging.   Now the truth struck into the soul of Abner.   "Hide yourself, Mary," he whispered. "It is a pirate ship!"   And almost at the same instant the young man and his wife laid themselves flat on the ground among the bushes, but they were very careful, each of them, to take a position which would allow them to peep out through the twigs and leaves upon the scene before them.

There seemed to be a good deal of commotion on board the black schooner, and very soon a large boat pushed off from her side, and the men in it began rowing rapidly toward the shore, apparently making for a spot on the beach, not far from the bluff on which Abner and Mary were concealed. " Let us get up and run," whispered Mary, trembling from head to toe. " They are pirates, and they are coming here ! "

" Lie still ! Lie still ! " said Abner. " If we get up and leave these bushes, we shall be seen, and then they will be after us ! Lie still, and do not move a finger ! "

The trembling Mary obeyed her husband, and they both lay quite still, scarcely breathing, with eyes wide open. The boat rapidly approached the shore. Abner counted ten men rowing and one man sitting in the stern. The boat seemed to be heavily loaded, and the oarsmen rowed hard.

Now the boat was run through the surf to the beach, and its eleven occupants jumped out. There was no mistaking their character. They were true pirates. They had great cutlasses and pistols, and one of them was very tall and broad shouldered, and wore an old-fashioned cocked hat.

" That's Captain Kidd," whispered Abner to his wife, and she pressed his hand to let him know that she thought he must be right.

" The boat was run through the surf to the beach." — p. 300.

Now the men came up high upon the beach, and began looking about here and there as if they were searching for something. Mary was filled with horror for fear they should come to that bluff to search, but Abner knew there was no danger of that. They had probably come to those shores to bury treasure, as if they were great sea-turtles coming up upon the beach to lay their eggs, and they were now looking for some good spot where they might dig.

Presently the tall man gave some orders in a low voice, and then his men left him to himself, and went back to the boat. There was a great pine tree standing back a considerable distance from the water, battered and racked by storms, but still a tough old tree. Toward this the pirate captain stalked, and standing close to it, with his back against it, he looked up into the sky. It was plain that he was looking for a star. There were very few of these luminaries to be seen in the heavens, for the moon was so bright. But as Abner looked in the direction in which the pirate captain gazed, he saw a star still bright in spite of the moonlight.

With his eyes fixed upon this star, the pirate captain now stepped forward, making long strides. One, two, three, four, five, six, seven. Then he stopped, plunged his right heel in the soft ground, and turned squarely about to the left, so that his

broad back was now parallel with a line drawn from
the pine tree to the star.

At right angles to this line the pirate now stepped
forward, making as before seven long paces. Then
he stopped, dug his heel into the ground, and beckoned to his men. Up they came running, carrying
picks and spades, and with great alacrity they began
to dig at the place where the captain had marked
with his heel.

It was plain that these pirates were used to making excavations, for it was not long before the hole
was so deep that those within it could not be
seen. Then the captain gave an order to cease
digging, and he and all the pirates went back to
the boat.

For about half an hour,—though Mary thought
it was a longer time than that,—those pirates
worked very hard carrying great boxes and bags
from the boat to the excavation. When everything
had been brought up, two of the pirates went down
into the hole, and the others handed to them the
various packages. Skilfully and quickly they worked,
doubtless storing their goods with great care, until
nearly everything which had been brought from the
boat had been placed in the deep hole. Some rolls
of goods were left upon the ground which Mary
thought were carpets, but which Abner believed to
be rich Persian rugs, or something of that kind.

"Two of the pirates went down into the hole." — p. 302.

Now the captain stepped aside, and picking up from the sand some little sticks and reeds, he selected ten of them, and with these in one hand, and with their ends protruding a short distance above his closed fingers, he rejoined his men. They gathered before him, and he held out toward them the hand which contained the little sticks.

"They're drawing lots!" gasped Abner, and Mary trembled more than she had done yet.

Now the lots were all drawn, and one man, apparently a young pirate, stepped out from among his fellows. His head was bowed, and his arms were folded across his manly chest. The captain spoke a few words, and the young pirate advanced alone to the side of the deep hole.

Mary now shut her eyes tight, tight; but Abner's were wide open. There was a sudden gleam of cutlasses in the air; there was one short, plaintive groan, and the body of the young pirate fell into the hole. Instantly all the other goods, furs, rugs, or whatever they were, were tumbled in upon him. Then the men began to shovel in the earth and sand, and in an incredibly short time the hole was filled up even with the ground about it.

Of course all the earth and sand which had been taken out of the hole could not now be put back into it. But these experienced treasure-hiders knew exactly what to do with it. A spadeful at a time, the soil which could not be replaced was carried to the sea, and thrown out into the water, and when the whole place had been carefully smoothed over, the pirates gathered sticks and stones, and little bushes, and great masses of wild cranberry vines, and scattered them about over the place so that it soon looked exactly like the rest of the beach about it.

Then the tall captain gave another low command, the pirates returned to their boat, it was pushed off, and rapidly rowed back to the schooner. Up came the anchor, up went the dark sails. The low, black schooner was put about, and very soon she was disappearing over the darkening waters, her black flag fluttering fiercely high above her.

" Now, let us run," whispered poor Mary, who, although she had not seen everything, imagined a great deal ; for as the pirates were getting into their boat she had opened her eyes and had counted them, and there were only nine beside the tall captain.

Abner thought that her advice was very good, and starting up out of the brushwood they hastened home as fast as their legs would carry them.

The next day Abner seemed to be a changed man. He had work to do, but he neglected it. Never had such a thing happened before ! For hours he sat in front of the house, looking up into the sky, counting one, two, three, four, five, six, seven. Then he would twist himself around on the little bench, and count seven more.

This worthy couple lived in a small house which had a large cellar, and during the afternoon of that day Abner busied himself in clearing out this cellar, and taking out of it everything which it had contained. His wife asked no questions. In her soul she knew what Abner was thinking about.

Supper was over, and most of the people in the village were thinking of going to bed, when Abner said to Mary, " Let us each take a spade, and I will carry a pail, and we will go out upon the beach for a walk. If any one should see us, they would think that we were going to dig for clams."

" Oh, no, dear Abner!" cried Mary. "We must not dig there! Think of that young pirate. Almost the first thing we would come to would be him!"

" I have thought of that," said Abner; "but do you not believe that the most Christian act that you and I could do would be to take him out and place him in a proper grave near by?"

" Oh, no!" exclaimed Mary, "do not say such a thing as that! Think of his ghost! They killed him and put him there, that his ghost might guard their treasure. You know, Abner, as well as I do, that this is their dreadful fashion!"

" I know all about that," said Abner, "and that is the reason I wish to go to-night. I do not believe there has yet been time enough for his ghost to form. But let us take him out now, dear Mary, and lay him reverently away, — and then!" He looked at her with flashing eyes.

"But, Abner," said she, "do you think we have the right?"

"Of course we have," said he. "Those treasures do not belong to the pirates. If we take them they are treasure-trove, and legally ours. And think, dear Mary, how poor we are to-night, and how rich we may be to-morrow! Come, get the pail. We must be off."

Running nearly all the way, — for they were in such a hurry they could not walk, — Abner and Mary soon reached the bluff, and hastily scrambling down to the beach below, they stood upon the dreadful spot where Captain Kidd and his pirates had stood the night before. There was the old battered pine tree, reaching out two of its bare arms encouragingly toward them.

Without loss of time Abner walked up to the tree, put his back to it, and then looked up into the sky. Now he called Mary to him. "Which star do you think he looked at, good wife?" said he. "There is a bright one low down, and then there is another one a little higher up, and farther to the right, but it is fainter."

"It would be the bright one, I think," said

Mary. And then Abner, his eyes fixed upon the bright star, commenced to stride. One, two, three, four, five, six, seven. Turning squarely around to the left he again made seven paces. And now he beckoned vigorously to Mary to come and dig.

For about ten minutes they dug, and then they laid bare a great mass of rock. "This isn't the place," cried Abner. "I must begin again. I did not look at the right star. I will take the other one."

For the greater part of that night Abner and Mary remained upon the beach. Abner would put his back against the tree, fix his eyes upon another star, stride forward seven paces, and then seven to the left, and he would come upon a little scrubby pine tree. Of course that was not the place.

The moon soon began to set, and more stars came out, so that Abner had a greater choice. Again and again he made his measurements, and every time that he came to the end of his second seven paces, he found that it would have been impossible for the pirates to make their excavation there.

There was clearly something wrong. Abner thought that he had not selected the right star, and Mary thought that his legs were not long enough. "That pirate captain," quoth she, "had a long and manly stride. Seven of his paces would go a far greater distance than seven of yours, Abner."

Abner made his paces a little longer; but although he and his wife kept up their work until they could see the early dawn, they found no spot where it would be worth while to dig, and so mournfully they returned to their home and their empty cellar.

As long as the moonlight lasted, Abner and Mary went to the little beach at the head of the bay, and made their measurements and their searches, but although they sometimes dug a little here and there, they always found that they had not struck the place where the pirate's treasure had been buried.

When at last they gave up their search, and concluded to put their household goods back into their cellar, they told the tale to some of the neighbors, and other people went out and dug, not only at the place which had been designated, but miles up and down the coast, and then the story was told and retold, and so it has lasted until the present day.

What has been said about the legendary Captain Kidd will give a very good idea of the estimation in which this romantic being has been, and still is, held in various parts of the country, and, of all the legitimate legends about him, there is not one which recounts his piratical deeds upon our coast. The reason for this will be seen when we consider, in the next chapter, the life and character of the real Captain Kidd.

# Chapter XXXII

## The Real Captain Kidd

WILLIAM KIDD, or Robert Kidd, as he is sometimes called, was a sailor in the merchant service who had a wife and family in New York. He was a very respectable man and had a good reputation as a seaman, and about 1690, when there was war between England and France, Kidd was given the command of a privateer, and having had two or three engagements with French vessels he showed himself to be a brave fighter and a prudent commander.

Some years later he sailed to England, and, while there, he received an appointment of a peculiar character. It was at the time when the King of England was doing his best to put down the pirates of the American coast, and Sir George Bellomont, the recently appointed Governor of New York, recommended Captain Kidd as a very suitable man to command a ship to be sent out to suppress piracy. When Kidd agreed to take the position of chief of marine police, he was not employed by

the Crown, but by a small company of gentlemen
of capital, who formed themselves into a sort of
trust company, or society for the prevention of cruelty to merchantmen, and the object of their associa-
tion was not only to put down pirates, but to put
some money in their own pockets as well.

Kidd was furnished with two commissions, one
appointing him a privateer with authority to capture
French vessels, and the other empowering him to
seize and destroy all pirate ships. Kidd was ordered
in his mission to keep a strict account of all booty
captured, in order that it might be fairly divided
among those who were stockholders in the enterprise, one-tenth of the total proceeds being reserved
for the King.

Kidd sailed from England in the *Adventure*, a
large ship with thirty guns and eighty men, and on
his way to America he captured a French ship
which he carried to New York. Here he arranged
to make his crew a great deal larger than had been
thought necessary in England, and, by offering a
fair share of the property he might confiscate on
piratical or French ships, he induced a great many
able seamen to enter his service, and when the *Adventure* left New York she carried a crew of one
hundred and fifty-five men.

With a fine ship and a strong crew, Kidd now
sailed out of the harbor with the ostensible purpose

of putting down piracy in American waters, but the methods of this legally appointed marine policeman were very peculiar, and, instead of cruising up and down our coast, he gayly sailed away to the island of Madeira, and then around the Cape of Good Hope to Madagascar and the Red Sea, thus getting himself as far out of his regular beat as any New York constable would have been had he undertaken to patrol the dominions of the Khan of Tartary.

By the time Captain Kidd reached that part of the world he had been at sea for nearly a year without putting down any pirates or capturing any French ships. In fact, he had made no money whatever for himself or the stockholders of the company which had sent him out. His men, of course, must have been very much surprised at this unusual neglect of his own and his employers' interests, but when he reached the Red Sea, he boldly informed them that he had made a change in his business, and had decided that he would be no longer a suppressor of piracy, but would become a pirate himself; and, instead of taking prizes of French ships only, — which he was legally empowered to do, — he would try to capture any valuable ship he could find on the seas, no matter to what nation it belonged. He then went on to state that his present purpose in coming into those oriental waters was to capture the rich fleet from Mocha

which was due in the lower part of the Red Sea
about that time.

The crew of the *Adventure*, who must have been
tired of having very little to do and making no
money, expressed their entire approbation of their
captain's change of purpose, and readily agreed to
become pirates.

Kidd waited a good while for the Mocha fleet,
but it did not arrive, and then he made his first
venture in actual piracy. He overhauled a Moor-
ish vessel which was commanded by an English
captain, and as England was not at war with
Morocco, and as the nationality of the ship's
commander should have protected him, Kidd thus
boldly broke the marine laws which governed the
civilized world and stamped himself an out-and-out
pirate. After the exercise of considerable cruelty
he extorted from his first prize a small amount of
money; and although he and his men did not gain
very much booty, they had whetted their appetites
for more, and Kidd cruised savagely over the
eastern seas in search of other spoils.

After a time the *Adventure* fell in with a fine
English ship, called the *Royal Captain*, and
although she was probably laden with a rich cargo,
Kidd did not attack her. His piratical character
was not yet sufficiently formed to give him the
disloyal audacity which would enable him with his

English ship and his English crew, to fall upon another English ship manned by another English crew. In time his heart might be hardened, but he felt that he could not begin with this sort of thing just yet. So the *Adventure* saluted the *Royal Captain* with ceremonious politeness, and each vessel passed quietly on its way. But this conscientious consideration did not suit Kidd's crew. They had already had a taste of booty, and they were hungry for more, and when the fine English vessel, of which they might so easily have made a prize, was allowed to escape them, they were loud in their complaints and grumblings.

One of the men, a gunner, named William Moore, became actually impertinent upon the subject, and he and Captain Kidd had a violent quarrel, in the course of which the captain picked up a heavy iron-bound bucket and struck the dissatisfied gunner on the head with it. The blow was such a powerful one that the man's skull was broken, and he died the next day.

Captain Kidd's conscience seems to have been a good deal in his way; for although he had been sailing about in various eastern waters, taking prizes wherever he could, he was anxious that reports of his misdeeds should not get home before him. Having captured a fine vessel bound westward, he took from her all the booty he could, and then proceeded to arrange matters so that the capture of this ship should appear to be a legal transaction. The ship was manned by Moors and commanded by a Dutchman, and of course Kidd had no right to touch it, but the sharp-witted and business-like pirate selected one of the passengers and made him sign a paper declaring that he was a Frenchman, and that he commanded the ship. When this statement had been sworn to before witnesses, Kidd put the document in his pocket so that if he were called upon to explain the transaction he might be able to show that he had good reason to suppose that he had captured a French ship, which, of course, was all right and proper.

Kidd now ravaged the East India waters with great success and profit, and at last he fell in with a very fine ship from Armenia, called the *Quedagh Merchant*, commanded by an Englishman. Kidd's conscience had been growing harder and harder every day, and he did not now hesitate to attack any vessel. The great merchantman was captured, and proved to be one of the most valuable prizes ever taken by a pirate, for Kidd's own share of the spoils amounted to more than sixty thousand dollars. This was such a grand haul that Kidd lost no time in taking his prize to some place where he might safely dispose of her cargo, and get rid of her passengers. Accordingly he sailed for Madagascar.

" The great merchantman was captured." — p. 314.

While he was there he fell in with the first pirate vessel he had met since he had started out to put down piracy. This was a ship commanded by an English pirate named Culliford, and here would have been a chance for Captain Kidd to show that, although he might transgress the law himself, he would be true to his engagement not to allow other people to do so; but he had given up putting down piracy, and instead of apprehending Culliford he went into partnership with him, and the two agreed to go pirating together.

This partnership, however, did not continue long, for Captain Kidd began to believe that it was time for him to return to his native country and make a report of his proceedings to his employers. Having confined his piratical proceedings to distant parts of the world, he hoped that he would be able to make Sir George Bellomont and the other stockholders suppose that his booty was all legitimately taken from French vessels cruising in the east, and when the proper division should be made he would be able to quietly enjoy his portion of the treasure he had gained.

He did not go back in the *Adventure*, which was probably not large enough to carry all the booty he had amassed, but putting everything on board his latest prize, the *Quedagh Merchant*, he burned his old ship and sailed homeward.

When he reached the West Indies, however, our wary sea-robber was very much surprised to find that accounts of his evil deeds had reached America, and that the colonial authorities had been so much incensed by the news that the man who had been sent out to suppress piracy had become himself a pirate, that they had circulated notices throughout the different colonies, urging the arrest of Kidd if he should come into any American port. This was disheartening intelligence for the treasure-laden Captain Kidd, but he did not despair; he knew that the love of money was often as strong in the minds of human beings as the love of justice. Sir George Bellomont, who was now in New York, was one of the principal stockholders in the enterprise, and Kidd hoped that the rich share of the results of his industry which would come to the Governor might cause unpleasant reports to be disregarded. In this case he might yet return to his wife and family with a neat little fortune, and without danger of being called upon to explain his exceptional performances in the eastern seas.

Of course Kidd was not so foolish and rash as to sail into New York harbor on board the *Quedagh Merchant*, so he bought a small sloop and put the most valuable portion of his goods on board her, leaving his larger vessel, which also contained a great quantity of merchandise, in the charge of one of his confederates, and in the little sloop he cautiously approached the coast of New Jersey. His great desire was to find out what sort of a reception he might expect, so he entered Delaware Bay, and when he stopped at a little seaport in order to take in some supplies, he discovered that there was but small chance of his visiting his home and his family, and of making a report to his superior in the character of a deserving mariner who had returned after a successful voyage. Some people in the village recognized him, and the report soon spread to New York that the pirate Kidd was lurking about the coast. A sloop of war was sent out to capture his vessel, and finding that it was impossible to remain in the vicinity where he had been discovered, Kidd sailed northward and entered Long Island Sound.

Here the shrewd and anxious pirate began to act the part of the watch dog who has been killing sheep. In every way he endeavored to assume the appearance of innocence and to conceal every sign of misbehavior. He wrote to Sir George Bellomont that he should have called upon him in order to report his proceedings and hand over his profits, were it not for the wicked and malicious reports which had been circulated about him.

It was during this period of suspense, when the returned pirate did not know what was likely to happen, that it is supposed, by the believers in the

hidden treasures of Kidd, that he buried his coin
and bullion and his jewels, some in one place and
some in another, so that if he were captured his
riches would not be taken with him. Among the
wild stories which were believed at that time, and
for long years after, was one to the effect that Captain Kidd's ship was chased up the Hudson River
by a man-of-war, and that the pirates, finding they
could not get away, sank their ship and fled to the
shore with all the gold and silver they could carry,
which they afterwards buried at the foot of Dunder-
bergh Mountain. A great deal of rocky soil has
been turned over at different times in search of
these treasures, but no discoveries of hidden coin
have yet been reported. The fact is, however, that
during this time of anxious waiting Kidd never
sailed west of Oyster Bay in Long Island. He was
afraid to approach New York, although he had frequent communication with that city, and was joined
by his wife and family.

About this time occurred an incident which has
given rise to all the stories regarding the buried
treasure of Captain Kidd. The disturbed and anxious pirate concluded that it was a dangerous thing
to keep so much valuable treasure on board his vessel which might at any time be overhauled by the
authorities, and he therefore landed at Gardiner's
Island on the Long Island coast, and obtained per-

mission from the proprietor to bury some of his superfluous stores upon his estate. This was a straightforward transaction. Mr. Gardiner knew all about the burial of the treasure, and when it was afterwards proved that Kidd was really a pirate the hidden booty was all given up to the government.

This appears to be the only case in which it was positively known that Kidd buried treasure on our coast, and it has given rise to all the stories of the kind which have ever been told.

For some weeks Kidd's sloop remained in Long Island Sound, and then he took courage and went to Boston to see some influential people there. He was allowed to go freely about the city for a week, and then he was arrested.

The rest of Kidd's story is soon told; he was sent to England for trial, and there he was condemned to death, not only for the piracies he had committed, but also for the murder of William Moore. He was executed, and his body was hung in chains on the banks of the Thames, where for years it dangled in the wind, a warning to all evil-minded sailors.

About the time of Kidd's trial and execution a ballad was written which had a wide circulation in England and America. It was set to music, and for many years helped to spread the fame of this pirate. The ballad was a very long one, containing

nearly twenty-six verses, and some of them run as
follows : —

> My name was Robert Kidd, when I sailed, when I sailed,
>    My name was Robert Kidd, when I sailed,
>       My name was Robert Kidd,
>          God's laws I did forbid,
> And so wickedly I did, when I sailed.

> My parents taught me well, when I sailed, when I sailed,
>    My parents taught me well when I sailed,
>       My parents taught me well
>          To shun the gates of hell,
> But 'gainst them I rebelled, when I sailed.

> I'd a Bible in my hand, when I sailed, when I sailed,
>    I'd a Bible in my hand when I sailed,
>       I'd a Bible in my hand,
>          By my father's great command,
> And sunk it in the sand, when I sailed.

> I murdered William Moore, as I sailed, as I sailed,
>    I murdered William Moore as I sailed,
>       I murdered William Moore,
>          And laid him in his gore,
> Not many leagues from shore, as I sailed.

> I was sick and nigh to death, when I sailed, when I sailed,
>    I was sick and nigh to death when I sailed,
>       I was sick and nigh to death,
>          And I vowed at every breath,
> To walk in wisdom's ways, as I sailed.

I thought I was undone, as I sailed, as I sailed,
    I thought I was undone, as I sailed,
        I thought I was undone,
            And my wicked glass had run,
But health did soon return, as I sailed.


My repentance lasted not, as I sailed, as I sailed,
    My repentance lasted not, as I sailed,
        My repentance lasted not,
            My vows I soon forgot,
Damnation was my lot, as I sailed.


I spyed the ships from France, as I sailed, as I sailed,
    I spyed the ships from France, as I sailed,
        I spyed the ships from France,
            To them I did advance,
And took them all by chance, as I sailed.


I spyed the ships of Spain, as I sailed, as I sailed,
    I spyed the ships of Spain, as I sailed,
        I spyed the ships of Spain,
            I fired on them amain,
'Till most of them was slain, as I sailed.


I'd ninety bars of gold, as I sailed, as I sailed,
    I'd ninety bars of gold, as I sailed,
        I'd ninety bars of gold,
            And dollars manifold,
With riches uncontrolled, as I sailed.


Thus being o'er-taken at last, I must die, I must die,
    Thus being o'er-taken at last, I must die,

Thus being o'er-taken at last,
And into prison cast,
And sentence being passed, I must die.


Farewell, the raging main, I must die, I must die,
Farewell, the raging main, I must die,
Farewell, the raging main,
To Turkey, France, and Spain,
I shall ne'er see you again, I must die.


To Execution Dock I must go, I must go,
To Execution Dock I must go,
To Execution Dock,
Will many thousands flock,
But I must bear the shock, and must die.


Come all ye young and old, see me die, see me die,
Come all ye young and old, see me die,
Come all ye young and old,
You're welcome to my gold,
For by it I've lost my soul, and must die.


Take warning now by me, for I must die, for I must die,
Take warning now by me, for I must die,
Take warning now by me,
And shun bad company,
Lest you come to hell with me, for I die.


It is said that Kidd showed no repentance when
he was tried, but insisted that he was the victim of
malicious persons who swore falsely against him.

And yet a more thoroughly dishonest rascal never sailed under the black flag. In the guise of an accredited officer of the government, he committed the crimes he was sent out to suppress; he deceived his men; he robbed and misused his fellow-countrymen and his friends, and he even descended to the meanness of cheating and despoiling the natives of the West India Islands, with whom he traded. These people were in the habit of supplying pirates with food and other necessaries, and they always found their rough customers entirely honest, and willing to pay for what they received; for as the pirates made a practice of stopping at certain points for supplies, they wished, of course, to be on good terms with those who furnished them. But Kidd had no ideas of honor toward people of high or low degree. He would trade with the natives as if he intended to treat them fairly and pay for all he got; but when the time came for him to depart, and he was ready to weigh anchor, he would seize upon all the commodities he could lay his hands upon, and without paying a copper to the distressed and indignant Indians, he would gayly sail away, his black flag flaunting derisively in the wind.

But although in reality Captain Kidd was no hero, he has been known for a century and more as the great American pirate, and his name has been representative of piracy ever since. Years after he had been hung, when people heard that a vessel with a black flag, or one which looked black in the distance, flying from its rigging had been seen, they forgot that the famous pirate was dead, and imagined that Captain Kidd was visiting their part of the coast in order that he might find a good place to bury some treasure which it was no longer safe for him to carry about.

There were two great reasons for the fame of Captain Kidd. One of these was the fact that he had been sent out by important officers of the crown who expected to share the profits of his legitimate operations, but who were supposed by their enemies to be perfectly willing to take any sort of profits provided it could not be proved that they were the results of piracy, and who afterwards allowed Kidd to suffer for their sins as well as his own. These opinions introduced certain political features into his career and made him a very much talked-of man. The greater reason for his fame, however, was the widespread belief in his buried treasures, and this made him the object of the most intense interest to hundreds of misguided people who hoped to be lucky enough to share his spoils.

There were other pirates on the American coast during the eighteenth century, and some of them became very well known, but their stories are not uncommon, and we need not tell them here. As our country became better settled, and as well-armed revenue cutters began to cruise up and down our Atlantic coast for the protection of our commerce, pirates became fewer and fewer, and even those who were still bold enough to ply their trade grew milder in their manners, less daring in their exploits, and — more important than anything else — so unsuccessful in their illegal enterprises that they were forced to admit that it was now more profitable to command or work a merchantman than endeavor to capture one, and so the sea-robbers of our coasts gradually passed away.

# A CATALOG OF SELECTED
# DOVER BOOKS
## IN ALL FIELDS OF INTEREST

# CATALOG OF DOVER BOOKS

STICKLEY CRAFTSMAN FURNITURE CATALOGS, Gustav Stickley and L. & J. G. Stickley. Beautiful, functional furniture in two authentic catalogs from 1910. 594 illustrations, including 277 photos, show settles, rockers, armchairs, reclining chairs, bookcases, desks, tables. 183pp. 6½ x 9¼. 0-486-23838-5

AMERICAN LOCOMOTIVES IN HISTORIC PHOTOGRAPHS: 1858 to 1949, Ron Ziel (ed.). A rare collection of 126 meticulously detailed official photographs, called "builder portraits," of American locomotives that majestically chronicle the rise of steam locomotive power in America. Introduction. Detailed captions. xi+129pp. 9 x 12. 0-486-27393-8

AMERICA'S LIGHTHOUSES: An Illustrated History, Francis Ross Holland, Jr. Delightfully written, profusely illustrated fact-filled survey of over 200 American lighthouses since 1716. History, anecdotes, technological advances, more. 240pp. 8 x 10¾. 0-486-25576-X

TOWARDS A NEW ARCHITECTURE, Le Corbusier. Pioneering manifesto by founder of "International School." Technical and aesthetic theories, views of industry, economics, relation of form to function, "mass-production split" and much more. Profusely illustrated. 320pp. 6⅛ x 9¼. (Available in U.S. only.) 0-486-25023-7

HOW THE OTHER HALF LIVES, Jacob Riis. Famous journalistic record, exposing poverty and degradation of New York slums around 1900, by major social reformer. 100 striking and influential photographs. 233pp. 10 x 7⅞. 0-486-22012-5

FRUIT KEY AND TWIG KEY TO TREES AND SHRUBS, William M. Harlow. One of the handiest and most widely used identification aids. Fruit key covers 120 deciduous and evergreen species; twig key 160 deciduous species. Easily used. Over 300 photographs. 126pp. 5⅜ x 8½. 0-486-20511-8

COMMON BIRD SONGS, Dr. Donald J. Borror. Songs of 60 most common U.S. birds: robins, sparrows, cardinals, bluejays, finches, more–arranged in order of increasing complexity. Up to 9 variations of songs of each species.
Cassette and manual 0-486-99911-4

ORCHIDS AS HOUSE PLANTS, Rebecca Tyson Northen. Grow cattleyas and many other kinds of orchids–in a window, in a case, or under artificial light. 63 illustrations. 148pp. 5⅜ x 8½. 0-486-23261-1

MONSTER MAZES, Dave Phillips. Masterful mazes at four levels of difficulty. Avoid deadly perils and evil creatures to find magical treasures. Solutions for all 32 exciting illustrated puzzles. 48pp. 8¼ x 11. 0-486-26005-4

MOZART'S DON GIOVANNI (DOVER OPERA LIBRETTO SERIES), Wolfgang Amadeus Mozart. Introduced and translated by Ellen H. Bleiler. Standard Italian libretto, with complete English translation. Convenient and thoroughly portable–an ideal companion for reading along with a recording or the performance itself. Introduction. List of characters. Plot summary. 121pp. 5¼ x 8½. 0-486-24944-1

FRANK LLOYD WRIGHT'S DANA HOUSE, Donald Hoffmann. Pictorial essay of residential masterpiece with over 160 interior and exterior photos, plans, elevations, sketches and studies. 128pp. 9¼ x 10¾. 0-486-29120-0

THE CLARINET AND CLARINET PLAYING, David Pino. Lively, comprehensive work features suggestions about technique, musicianship, and musical interpretation, as well as guidelines for teaching, making your own reeds, and preparing for public performance. Includes an intriguing look at clarinet history. "A godsend," *The Clarinet,* Journal of the International Clarinet Society. Appendixes. 7 illus. 320pp. $5\frac{3}{8}$ x $8\frac{1}{2}$. 0-486-40270-3

HOLLYWOOD GLAMOR PORTRAITS, John Kobal (ed.). 145 photos from 1926-49. Harlow, Gable, Bogart, Bacall; 94 stars in all. Full background on photographers, technical aspects. 160pp. $8\frac{3}{8}$ x $11\frac{1}{4}$. 0-486-23352-9

THE RAVEN AND OTHER FAVORITE POEMS, Edgar Allan Poe. Over 40 of the author's most memorable poems: "The Bells," "Ulalume," "Israfel," "To Helen," "The Conqueror Worm," "Eldorado," "Annabel Lee," many more. Alphabetic lists of titles and first lines. 64pp. $5\frac{3}{16}$ x $8\frac{1}{4}$. 0-486-26685-0

PERSONAL MEMOIRS OF U. S. GRANT, Ulysses Simpson Grant. Intelligent, deeply moving firsthand account of Civil War campaigns, considered by many the finest military memoirs ever written. Includes letters, historic photographs, maps and more. 528pp. $6\frac{1}{8}$ x $9\frac{1}{4}$. 0-486-28587-1

ANCIENT EGYPTIAN MATERIALS AND INDUSTRIES, A. Lucas and J. Harris. Fascinating, comprehensive, thoroughly documented text describes this ancient civilization's vast resources and the processes that incorporated them in daily life, including the use of animal products, building materials, cosmetics, perfumes and incense, fibers, glazed ware, glass and its manufacture, materials used in the mummification process, and much more. 544pp. $6^1/_8$ x $9^1/_4$. (Available in U.S. only.) 0-486-40446-3

RUSSIAN STORIES/RUSSKIE RASSKAZY: A Dual-Language Book, edited by Gleb Struve. Twelve tales by such masters as Chekhov, Tolstoy, Dostoevsky, Pushkin, others. Excellent word-for-word English translations on facing pages, plus teaching and study aids, Russian/English vocabulary, biographical/critical introductions, more. 416pp. $5\frac{3}{8}$ x $8\frac{1}{2}$. 0-486-26244-8

PHILADELPHIA THEN AND NOW: 60 Sites Photographed in the Past and Present, Kenneth Finkel and Susan Oyama. Rare photographs of City Hall, Logan Square, Independence Hall, Betsy Ross House, other landmarks juxtaposed with contemporary views. Captures changing face of historic city. Introduction. Captions. 128pp. $8\frac{1}{4}$ x 11. 0-486-25790-8

NORTH AMERICAN INDIAN LIFE: Customs and Traditions of 23 Tribes, Elsie Clews Parsons (ed.). 27 fictionalized essays by noted anthropologists examine religion, customs, government, additional facets of life among the Winnebago, Crow, Zuni, Eskimo, other tribes. 480pp. $6\frac{1}{8}$ x $9\frac{1}{4}$. 0-486-27377-6

TECHNICAL MANUAL AND DICTIONARY OF CLASSICAL BALLET, Gail Grant. Defines, explains, comments on steps, movements, poses and concepts. 15-page pictorial section. Basic book for student, viewer. 127pp. $5\frac{3}{8}$ x $8\frac{1}{2}$. 0-486-21843-0

THE MALE AND FEMALE FIGURE IN MOTION: 60 Classic Photographic Sequences, Eadweard Muybridge. 60 true-action photographs of men and women walking, running, climbing, bending, turning, etc., reproduced from rare 19th-century masterpiece. vi + 121pp. 9 x 12. 0-486-24745-7

FRENCH STORIES/CONTES FRANÇAIS: A Dual-Language Book, Wallace Fowlie. Ten stories by French masters, Voltaire to Camus: "Micromegas" by Voltaire; "The Atheist's Mass" by Balzac; "Minuet" by de Maupassant; "The Guest" by Camus, six more. Excellent English translations on facing pages. Also French-English vocabulary list, exercises, more. 352pp. 5⅜ x 8½. 0-486-26443-2

CHICAGO AT THE TURN OF THE CENTURY IN PHOTOGRAPHS: 122 Historic Views from the Collections of the Chicago Historical Society, Larry A. Viskochil. Rare large-format prints offer detailed views of City Hall, State Street, the Loop, Hull House, Union Station, many other landmarks, circa 1904-1913. Introduction. Captions. Maps. 144pp. 9⅜ x 12¼. 0-486-24656-6

OLD BROOKLYN IN EARLY PHOTOGRAPHS, 1865-1929, William Lee Younger. Luna Park, Gravesend race track, construction of Grand Army Plaza, moving of Hotel Brighton, etc. 157 previously unpublished photographs. 165pp. 8⅞ x 11¾. 0-486-23587-4

THE MYTHS OF THE NORTH AMERICAN INDIANS, Lewis Spence. Rich anthology of the myths and legends of the Algonquins, Iroquois, Pawnees and Sioux, prefaced by an extensive historical and ethnological commentary. 36 illustrations. 480pp. 5⅜ x 8½. 0-486-25967-6

AN ENCYCLOPEDIA OF BATTLES: Accounts of Over 1,560 Battles from 1479 B.C. to the Present, David Eggenberger. Essential details of every major battle in recorded history from the first battle of Megiddo in 1479 B.C. to Grenada in 1984. List of Battle Maps. New Appendix covering the years 1967-1984. Index. 99 illustrations. 544pp. 6½ x 9¼. 0-486-24913-1

SAILING ALONE AROUND THE WORLD, Captain Joshua Slocum. First man to sail around the world, alone, in small boat. One of great feats of seamanship told in delightful manner. 67 illustrations. 294pp. 5⅜ x 8½. 0-486-20326-3

ANARCHISM AND OTHER ESSAYS, Emma Goldman. Powerful, penetrating, prophetic essays on direct action, role of minorities, prison reform, puritan hypocrisy, violence, etc. 271pp. 5⅜ x 8½. 0-486-22484-8

MYTHS OF THE HINDUS AND BUDDHISTS, Ananda K. Coomaraswamy and Sister Nivedita. Great stories of the epics; deeds of Krishna, Shiva, taken from puranas, Vedas, folk tales; etc. 32 illustrations. 400pp. 5⅜ x 8½. 0-486-21759-0

MY BONDAGE AND MY FREEDOM, Frederick Douglass. Born a slave, Douglass became outspoken force in antislavery movement. The best of Douglass' autobiographies. Graphic description of slave life. 464pp. 5⅜ x 8½. 0-486-22457-0

FOLLOWING THE EQUATOR: A Journey Around the World, Mark Twain. Fascinating humorous account of 1897 voyage to Hawaii, Australia, India, New Zealand, etc. Ironic, bemused reports on peoples, customs, climate, flora and fauna, politics, much more. 197 illustrations. 720pp. 5⅜ x 8½. 0-486-26113-1

THE PEOPLE CALLED SHAKERS, Edward D. Andrews. Definitive study of Shakers: origins, beliefs, practices, dances, social organization, furniture and crafts, etc. 33 illustrations. 351pp. 5⅜ x 8½. 0-486-21081-2

THE MYTHS OF GREECE AND ROME, H. A. Guerber. A classic of mythology, generously illustrated, long prized for its simple, graphic, accurate retelling of the principal myths of Greece and Rome, and for its commentary on their origins and significance. With 64 illustrations by Michelangelo, Raphael, Titian, Rubens, Canova, Bernini and others. 480pp. 5⅜ x 8½. 0-486-27584-1

HOW TO DO BEADWORK, Mary White. Fundamental book on craft from simple projects to five-bead chains and woven works. 106 illustrations. 142pp. 5⅜ x 8. 0-486-20697-1

THE 1912 AND 1915 GUSTAV STICKLEY FURNITURE CATALOGS, Gustav Stickley. With over 200 detailed illustrations and descriptions, these two catalogs are essential reading and reference materials and identification guides for Stickley furniture. Captions cite materials, dimensions and prices. 112pp. 6½ x 9¼. 0-486-26676-1

EARLY AMERICAN LOCOMOTIVES, John H. White, Jr. Finest locomotive engravings from early 19th century: historical (1804–74), main-line (after 1870), special, foreign, etc. 147 plates. 142pp. 11⅜ x 8¼. 0-486-22772-3

LITTLE BOOK OF EARLY AMERICAN CRAFTS AND TRADES, Peter Stockham (ed.). 1807 children's book explains crafts and trades: baker, hatter, cooper, potter, and many others. 23 copperplate illustrations. 140pp. 4⅝ x 6. 0-486-23336-7

VICTORIAN FASHIONS AND COSTUMES FROM HARPER'S BAZAR, 1867–1898, Stella Blum (ed.). Day costumes, evening wear, sports clothes, shoes, hats, other accessories in over 1,000 detailed engravings. 320pp. 9⅜ x 12¼. 0-486-22990-4

THE LONG ISLAND RAIL ROAD IN EARLY PHOTOGRAPHS, Ron Ziel. Over 220 rare photos, informative text document origin ( 1844) and development of rail service on Long Island. Vintage views of early trains, locomotives, stations, passengers, crews, much more. Captions. 8⅞ x 11¾. 0-486-26301-0

VOYAGE OF THE LIBERDADE, Joshua Slocum. Great 19th-century mariner's thrilling, first-hand account of the wreck of his ship off South America, the 35-foot boat he built from the wreckage, and its remarkable voyage home. 128pp. 5⅜ x 8½. 0-486-40022-0

TEN BOOKS ON ARCHITECTURE, Vitruvius. The most important book ever written on architecture. Early Roman aesthetics, technology, classical orders, site selection, all other aspects. Morgan translation. 331pp. 5⅜ x 8½. 0-486-20645-9

THE HUMAN FIGURE IN MOTION, Eadweard Muybridge. More than 4,500 stopped-action photos, in action series, showing undraped men, women, children jumping, lying down, throwing, sitting, wrestling, carrying, etc. 390pp. 7⅞ x 10⅝. 0-486-20204-6 Clothbd.

TREES OF THE EASTERN AND CENTRAL UNITED STATES AND CANADA, William M. Harlow. Best one-volume guide to 140 trees. Full descriptions, woodlore, range, etc. Over 600 illustrations. Handy size. 288pp. 4½ x 6⅜. 0-486-20395-6

GROWING AND USING HERBS AND SPICES, Milo Miloradovich. Versatile handbook provides all the information needed for cultivation and use of all the herbs and spices available in North America. 4 illustrations. Index. Glossary. 236pp. 5⅜ x 8½. 0-486-25058-X

BIG BOOK OF MAZES AND LABYRINTHS, Walter Shepherd. 50 mazes and labyrinths in all–classical, solid, ripple, and more–in one great volume. Perfect inexpensive puzzler for clever youngsters. Full solutions. 112pp. 8⅛ x 11. 0-486-22951-3

PIANO TUNING, J. Cree Fischer. Clearest, best book for beginner, amateur. Simple repairs, raising dropped notes, tuning by easy method of flattened fifths. No previous skills needed. 4 illustrations. 201pp. 5⅜ x 8½. 0-486-23267-0

HINTS TO SINGERS, Lillian Nordica. Selecting the right teacher, developing confidence, overcoming stage fright, and many other important skills receive thoughtful discussion in this indispensible guide, written by a world-famous diva of four decades' experience. 96pp. 5⅜ x 8½. 0-486-40094-8

THE COMPLETE NONSENSE OF EDWARD LEAR, Edward Lear. All nonsense limericks, zany alphabets, Owl and Pussycat, songs, nonsense botany, etc., illustrated by Lear. Total of 320pp. 5⅜ x 8½. (Available in U.S. only.) 0-486-20167-8

VICTORIAN PARLOUR POETRY: An Annotated Anthology, Michael R. Turner. 117 gems by Longfellow, Tennyson, Browning, many lesser-known poets. "The Village Blacksmith," "Curfew Must Not Ring Tonight," "Only a Baby Small," dozens more, often difficult to find elsewhere. Index of poets, titles, first lines. xxiii + 325pp. 5⅝ x 8¼. 0-486-27044-0

DUBLINERS, James Joyce. Fifteen stories offer vivid, tightly focused observations of the lives of Dublin's poorer classes. At least one, "The Dead," is considered a masterpiece. Reprinted complete and unabridged from standard edition. 160pp. 5$\frac{3}{16}$ x 8¼. 0-486-26870-5

GREAT WEIRD TALES: 14 Stories by Lovecraft, Blackwood, Machen and Others, S. T. Joshi (ed.). 14 spellbinding tales, including "The Sin Eater," by Fiona McLeod, "The Eye Above the Mantel," by Frank Belknap Long, as well as renowned works by R. H. Barlow, Lord Dunsany, Arthur Machen, W. C. Morrow and eight other masters of the genre. 256pp. 5⅜ x 8½. (Available in U.S. only.) 0-486-40436-6

THE BOOK OF THE SACRED MAGIC OF ABRAMELIN THE MAGE, translated by S. MacGregor Mathers. Medieval manuscript of ceremonial magic. Basic document in Aleister Crowley, Golden Dawn groups. 268pp. 5⅜ x 8½. 0-486-23211-5

THE BATTLES THAT CHANGED HISTORY, Fletcher Pratt. Eminent historian profiles 16 crucial conflicts, ancient to modern, that changed the course of civilization. 352pp. 5⅜ x 8½. 0-486-41129-X

NEW RUSSIAN-ENGLISH AND ENGLISH-RUSSIAN DICTIONARY, M. A. O'Brien. This is a remarkably handy Russian dictionary, containing a surprising amount of information, including over 70,000 entries. 366pp. 4½ x 6⅛. 0-486-20208-9

NEW YORK IN THE FORTIES, Andreas Feininger. 162 brilliant photographs by the well-known photographer, formerly with *Life* magazine. Commuters, shoppers, Times Square at night, much else from city at its peak. Captions by John von Hartz. 181pp. 9¼ x 10¾. 0-486-23585-8

INDIAN SIGN LANGUAGE, William Tomkins. Over 525 signs developed by Sioux and other tribes. Written instructions and diagrams. Also 290 pictographs. 111pp. 6⅛ x 9¼. 0-486-22029-X

ANATOMY: A Complete Guide for Artists, Joseph Sheppard. A master of figure drawing shows artists how to render human anatomy convincingly. Over 460 illustrations. 224pp. 8⅜ x 11¼. 0-486-27279-6

MEDIEVAL CALLIGRAPHY: Its History and Technique, Marc Drogin. Spirited history, comprehensive instruction manual covers 13 styles (ca. 4th century through 15th). Excellent photographs; directions for duplicating medieval techniques with modern tools. 224pp. 8⅜ x 11¼. 0-486-26142-5

## *CATALOG OF DOVER BOOKS*

LIGHT AND SHADE: A Classic Approach to Three-Dimensional Drawing, Mrs. Mary P. Merrifield. Handy reference clearly demonstrates principles of light and shade by revealing effects of common daylight, sunshine, and candle or artificial light on geometrical solids. 13 plates. 64pp. 5⅜ x 8½. 0-486-44143-1

ASTROLOGY AND ASTRONOMY: A Pictorial Archive of Signs and Symbols, Ernst and Johanna Lehner. Treasure trove of stories, lore, and myth, accompanied by more than 300 rare illustrations of planets, the Milky Way, signs of the zodiac, comets, meteors, and other astronomical phenomena. 192pp. 8⅜ x 11. 0-486-43981-X

JEWELRY MAKING: Techniques for Metal, Tim McCreight. Easy-to-follow instructions and carefully executed illustrations describe tools and techniques, use of gems and enamels, wire inlay, casting, and other topics. 72 line illustrations and diagrams. 176pp. 8¼ x 10⅞. 0-486-44043-5

MAKING BIRDHOUSES: Easy and Advanced Projects, Gladstone Califf. Easy-to-follow instructions include diagrams for everything from a one-room house for bluebirds to a forty-two-room structure for purple martins. 56 plates; 4 figures. 80pp. 8¾ x 6⅜. 0-486-44183-0

LITTLE BOOK OF LOG CABINS: How to Build and Furnish Them, William S. Wicks. Handy how-to manual, with instructions and illustrations for building cabins in the Adirondack style, fireplaces, stairways, furniture, beamed ceilings, and more. 102 line drawings. 96pp. 8¾ x 6⅜. 0-486-44259-4

THE SEASONS OF AMERICA PAST, Eric Sloane. From "sugaring time" and strawberry picking to Indian summer and fall harvest, a whole year's activities described in charming prose and enhanced with 79 of the author's own illustrations. 160pp. 8¼ x 11. 0-486-44220-9

THE METROPOLIS OF TOMORROW, Hugh Ferriss. Generous, prophetic vision of the metropolis of the future, as perceived in 1929. Powerful illustrations of towering structures, wide avenues, and rooftop parks–all features in many of today's modern cities. 59 illustrations. 144pp. 8¼ x 11. 0-486-43727-2

THE PATH TO ROME, Hilaire Belloc. This 1902 memoir abounds in lively vignettes from a vanished time, recounting a pilgrimage on foot across the Alps and Apennines in order to "see all Europe which the Christian Faith has saved." 77 of the author's original line drawings complement his sparkling prose. 272pp. 5⅜ x 8½. 0-486-44001-X

THE HISTORY OF RASSELAS: Prince of Abissinia, Samuel Johnson. Distinguished English writer attacks eighteenth-century optimism and man's unrealistic estimates of what life has to offer. 112pp. 5⅜ x 8½. 0-486-44094-X

A VOYAGE TO ARCTURUS, David Lindsay. A brilliant flight of pure fancy, where wild creatures crowd the fantastic landscape and demented torturers dominate victims with their bizarre mental powers. 272pp. 5⅜ x 8½. 0-486-44198-9

Paperbound unless otherwise indicated. Available at your book dealer, online at **www.doverpublications.com**, or by writing to Dept. GI, Dover Publications, Inc., 31 East 2nd Street, Mineola, NY 11501. For current price information or for free catalogs (please indicate field of interest), write to Dover Publications or log on to **www.doverpublications.com** and see every Dover book in print. Dover publishes more than 500 books each year on science, elementary and advanced mathematics, biology, music, art, literary history, social sciences, and other areas.